Uncensored Prayer

The Spiritual Practice of Wrestling With God

Uncensored Prayer

The Spiritual Practice of Wrestling With God

by Joy Wilson

CivitasPress
Publishing inspiring and redemptive ideas.™

Copyright Notice

Uncensored Prayer: The Spiritual Practice of Wrestling With God
© 2011 Civitas Press LLC
All Rights Reserved

Printed in the United States of America

ISBN # 978-0615480817 (Civitas Press)
Published by Civitas Press, LLC
Folsom, CA.
www.civitaspress.com

LCCN # 2011932390

Holy Bible, New Living Translation copyright © 1996, 2004, 2007 by Tyndale House Foundation. Used by permission of Tyndale House Publishers Inc., Carol Stream, Illinois 60188. All rights reserved. New Living, NLT, and the New Living Translation logo are registered trademarks of Tyndale House Publishers.

Scripture taken from the HOLY BIBLE, NEW INTERNATIONAL VERSION®. Copyright © 1973, 1978, 1984 Biblica. Used by permission of Zondervan. All rights reserved. The "NIV" and "New International Version" trademarks are registered in the United States Patent and Trademark Office by Biblica. Use of either trademark requires the permission of Biblica.

"Scripture taken from the *NEW AMERICAN STANDARD BIBLE*®, © Copyright 1960, 1962, 1963, 1968, 1971, 1972, 1973, 1975, 1977, 1995 by The Lockman Foundation. Used by permission. www.Lockman.org .

Contents

Acknowledgments	8
Introduction	9
SECTION 1 - PREPARING TO GET ON THE MAT	15
Chapter 1 - How To Know We're Hearing From God	17
Chapter 2 - Learning From Jacob	27
Chapter 3 - What We Gain By Wrestling With God	44
Chapter 4 - The Cost Of Wrestling With God	63
SECTION 2 - GETTING ON THE MAT	74
Chapter 5 - Letting Go Of Dishonesty	76
Chapter 6 - Learning To Wrestle	91
Chapter 7 - The No Fail Fall	103
Chapter 8 - Daddy God	110
Chapter 9 - Love And Acceptance	121
Chapter 10 - Helping Others	132
Chapter 11 - God Is My Co-Author	143
Chapter 12 - Quitting The Quitting	154
Chapter 13 - Pain	169
Chapter 14 - Grace	181
Chapter 15 - Addiction	189
Chapter 16 - Friends	205
Chapter 17 - We Are The Church	216
Epilogue - Reflections Of A Wrestler	225
Practical Applications	231

How To Support Joy Wilson

At Civitas Press, we believe in the power of social networking to help get the word out. As a reader of this book, we appreciate your voice in helping Joy spread the word about her work. If you would like to support Joy and help promote this book, please consider the following options:

1. Recommend this book to those in your social network, church, community, work or class;
2. Review the book on Amazon;
3. Share a link to the book on Facebook or Twitter;
4. Give the book to a friend who could help spread the word;
5. Email those in your personal or professional network with information about the book and a link to Amazon;
6. Blog about the book and provide a link to Amazon;
7. Recommend the book to your book club.

Please feel free to contact Joy Willson for interviews, media relations, guest blog posts, and speaking engagements. You can contact Joy at: joyleewilson@gmail.com.

Dedication

To the One who made me a wordsmith

and co-authored this book with me

Acknowledgments

To all the rings in my tree – every life experience, loss, pain, gain. I wouldn't be who I am today without all that has gone before.

To my parents, Jim and Nona Smith, who first had the pleasure and challenge of my company. I have not always been an easy child to raise, and I brought them much joy and concern. The biggest proof of their love is they never gave up on me, never stopped claiming me for God, and always believed that one day God would be the most important person in my life, and I would follow Him. Thank you so much.

To my children: Grace, Gideon, and Gabriel. I am so glad God gave you to me. We've been through some very dark times together, but many more wonderful times. I'm grateful that we are still close, and I love you with all my heart.

To all the friends who have never let me go. I've got your back, as you have mine.

To Heartsong Church and Pastor Steve Stone, a true friend. I am delighted to be a part of this tribe of Jesus-followers.

To all Outlaw Preachers, the first group who heard me read some of my most off-the-edge poems and said, "Yep, you're one of us. Welcome!"

To Connie Waters, one brave woman, and my editor, Jonathan Brink with Civitas Press – two fellow Outlaw Preachers who jointly pulled me and my poetry out from under a rock. Your support and love sustain me and my vision.

To Bud, my husband and love of my life. We've survived hell and enjoy eternal life together. We are committed to God and each other, and are one heck of a team, life-long hippies to the core. Thank you for affirming my calling as a wordsmith, and loving me, no matter what.

Best of all, thanks be to God, my wrestling partner.

Introduction

This is a book about the spiritual practice of wrestling with God by engaging in Uncensored Prayer. To wrestle with God is to argue with Him, risking honesty to gain intimacy, and naming our deepest fears. God wants to share Uncensored Prayer with everyone, talking about what we think and feel. It's wrestling through anger, faith, pain, hope, and what it means to be human. Winning is not the point. Restoration of love and trust is.

Wrestling with God is not about religion. Religion has nothing to do with this practice. Religion demands we bow our heads in subjection to a set of rules and regulations that tell us we're not good enough for God. Wrestling allows us to lift our heads in dignity, as we embrace the unconditional love of God for us. We struggle with Him out of relationship, not duty.

An amazing thing happens when we struggle with God. He shouts, "YES!" God longs to share uncensored dialogues with us; no subject, language, or feeling is unholy. In Peter Rollins' book, *The Fidelity of Betrayal*, he writes, *"Commitment to God involves a deep and sustained wrestling with God"*... by *"people who demonstrate their love and commitment to the source of their faith in a radical commitment to fighting with that source."*[1] As Peter suggests, wrestling with God assumes a commitment to God with faith in our source of life.

I have wrestled with God since I was a teenager, alternating between what I thought was the "right" way to pray and just plain yelling at Him. The wrestling grew out of traumatic experiences with males who promised love but instead delivered pain. I mistakenly thought God was one of them.

---

1 Peter Rollins, *The Fidelity of Betrayal* (Brewster, MA: Paraclete Press, 2008), 32.

I used to believe I could hide truth from God about things that caused me shame. If I didn't talk about it in prayer, He wouldn't know, even though I also believed God already knew what I was thinking. I came to realize I was the one who needed to be honest about the realities in my life.

While I initially believed God heard my prayers, I couldn't hear His voice until I removed the barriers I had erected that supposedly protected me, until I screamed out the years of compressed pain. I took the risk to trust God with Uncensored Prayer. And then a funny thing happened. God let me have it, yelling back His love for me. And in this process, my relationship with God was transformed.

Today our relationship is like a father to daughter. God holds me in His arms and protects me while encouraging me to grow. I am His child, finding my strength and courage from the love He provides. We laugh, cry, and occasionally scream together, wrestling in the dirt when that's what I need, because I can't do that with anyone else without offending them. God is incapable of being shocked or offended by anything I throw at Him. He is truth Himself, and values truth from me. God is not afraid of anything I can say or do. Prayer *can* be uncensored. This is the kind of relationship God wants, not just with me, but also with everyone. The question is how often do we engage it.

This book will explore the intimate conversations between God and myself. I share them with you to invite you into that space of wrestling, and to free yourself from the limitations you've created. God is bigger than we can ever imagine and can handle our deepest fears, harsh words, and intimate thoughts.

Many of us have been taught to talk "at" God, saying things we think God wants to hear. Or the only way we know how to pray is by reading communal prayers out of a book at church or following a defined script. There are hundreds of books and seminars to teach us the "right" way to pray. But Jesus' disciples asked *him* to teach them about prayer. Unfortunately, we've taken "the Lord's Prayer" as a mantra, as if "that's all there is, folks." Most of the other prayers in the Bible we can't imagine ourselves praying. Why? They aren't ours. And while Jesus' instructions for prayer are vital, giving us a starting point for prayer, Uncensored Prayer is about discovering our own words.

This book is then an invitation to engage in the practice of wrestling with God through Uncensored Prayer. Perhaps you have a loving relationship with God, but your prayers are limited by traditions about what's appropriate to say. Or you may question everything religious and think prayer is a "four-letter word," having been wounded or marginalized by the church. I encourage you to throw caution to the wind and let all of your preconceived notions go. Consider trying the spiritual practice of uncensored dialogues with God for yourself.

At the foot of God's throne is a wrestling mat. Try it out.

Joy Wilson

The Screw Ups

I screw up really bad several days a week
Is that normal?

No, but...

I knew it!
I'm weird and worse than everybody else.

*You didn't let me finish
(that was very dramatic, by the way).
Screwing up weekly is normal for you and everyone else, too.
Hate to break your all or nothing thinking,
but your mistakes aren't all that special.*

What?

*You're special, but not better or worse than other people.
I came to save the world, not just you.
I didn't teach you your misinformation;
you learned it from others, not me.
It's a lie that you're a loser.
I keep trying to tell you that, but you won't listen.*

I get really bummed out when I make a bad mistake.
I can handle the little ones, but not those.

*That's why you need me –
to experience grace you obviously can't give yourself.
I don't just see your potential,
but the majority marvelous things about you.
I never bother to make mistakes.
I'm a professional artist, proud of all my creation.
Give yourself a break, child; everyone is abnormal,
meaning each person, cow, and rock are uniquely different,
which was a lot more fun to make than repetition.*

I love talking with you,
because I lose my perspective
and your perspective is...well, so odd.

That's because I'm uniquely different, too.

I'm glad you have your job instead of me.

Me, too.

SECTION 1

PREPARING TO GET ON THE MAT

I am often asked, "How did I begin to wrestle with God? How did I learn to get on the mat with God?" To really answer that question, I have to begin with another question. When did I start my relationship with God? David suggests before I was born.

> *Yet You are He who brought me forth from the womb; You made me trust when upon my mother's breasts. Upon You I was cast from birth; You have been my God from my mother's womb.* Psalm 22:9-10 (NASB)

The Psalms suggest that God knew everything about me before I was born – literally everything. So there was essentially nothing I could hide from God. The only person then who needed to face the truth was me. Learning to wrestle was just as much about getting honest with myself as in admitting it to God.

Actually, I fell into the practice of wrestling with God. After years of trying to pray the way everyone else had taught me, I reached a point of admitting it just didn't work for me. I needed my own words. So I just decided to trust that God could handle my fears, my issues, my failures, and my doubts. And so I wrestled.

Children are born with a natural sense of trust, but life experiences change that. At some point in our lives, we discover our parents are fallible and God doesn't always give us what we want. As a young adult, I thought that meant there was something wrong with me or with the way I prayed. Then I learned at church the "appropriate" way to pray. I was to close my eyes, bow my head in reverence, and pray silently. I could ask God for things, but only the things I was supposed to have, and I wasn't sure what that was at times. It honestly didn't work. I felt like God was up there and I was down here. Eventually I gave up trying, but I never lost the awful feeling that there was a chasm between God and me, and it was my fault. Sometimes I tried being a "good girl", seeking God's approval, and not knowing I already had it. Other times, I shouted "at" God about how unfair He was. I believed God heard me, but that was it.

About twenty years ago, the sense of disconnection from God hurt badly enough for me to ask Him to show up and fight fair, and He did. Not really knowing how to pray, I got mad at God. I chose to give Him a piece of my mind. But I was also ready to listen. So we started a conversation. It wasn't pretty, but it was real. I began to realize that God had been talking to me all my life. I just didn't have ears to hear yet. I hadn't yet learned that I needed to practice listening. The more we shared Uncensored Prayer, the more I heard Him in a variety of ways.

In this first section, I want to begin preparing you for wrestling with God in Uncensored Prayer. Getting on the mat is an incredible experience, but it is also scary. To help engage you in the experience, we'll explore some of the critical ideas behind wrestling that include: *How to know you are hearing from God, learning how to wrestle from Jacob's experience, what we gain by wrestling with God, and the cost of wrestling with God.*

The first step into Uncensored Prayer begins with trust. It begins with taking the risk to engage God in conversation by sharing your heart AND listening. What follows is not just a dialogue of prayer but also practical steps to engaging that dialogue for yourself. Are you ready?

Chapter 1

How To Know We're Hearing From God

If you're like me, learning to pray can seem like a scary journey. Our imagination can get the best of us before we've even started. Will we say the right things? Will God even listen? How do we even know we're hearing from God? And once we do, believing that we can say anything to God can actually seem like irreverence. But I assure you it's not. It's the highest form of trust.

So how do we know if it's God's voice? Uncensored Prayer requires taking the risk to believe God is actually speaking to us, and then requires listening to God. It requires stepping into trust and actually believing in what we hear. God will respond if we are listening. Trusting that it is can seems so scary. It requires believing that God is actually there, waiting to speak.

To support your own journey into Uncensored Prayer, I want to give you four things to consider when listening to God: *Ask God to know it's Him talking, God reveals things we don't know, confirmation from Scripture, and confirmation from others.*

Ask God To Know It's Him Talking

It can be especially confusing when you're first trying Uncensored Prayer, to know if God's talking to you or if you're making it up in your head. But remember: God wants you to find Him and to hear Him. We just have to be willing to listen.

> *But if from there you will seek (inquire for and require as necessity) the Lord your God, you will find Him if you [truly]*

> seek Him with all your heart [and mind] and soul and life.
> Deuteronomy 4:29 (AMP)

When we engage God in relationship, when we seek out His voice, we can ask God for proof that we actually heard from Him.

> "I will open the windows of heaven for you. I will pour out a blessing so great you won't have enough room to take it in! Try it! Put me to the test!" Malachi 3:10 (NLT)

So then, what if you ask, and you feel stupid, because you don't feel like you heard anything from God. Did you do it wrong? Was God really listening? Maybe this wasn't such a great idea. Learning to engage in Uncensored Prayer often takes time.

My oldest son, Gideon, loves playing basketball and is good at it. Throughout his youth he played for a competitive club team. His first year of high school, Gideon tried out for the freshman basketball team and made it. This was the last year he was eligible for his competitive team, where he was a successful, respected player. Who knew how he would do on the school team, facing new challenges, but his future was in his high school basketball team.

The problem was Gideon couldn't play on both teams at once. He had to choose between them. With a deadline staring him in the face, I told him to ask God to make the right choice clear.

My son had never sought God's will before, and was skeptical, but gave it a try anyway. Knowing him, I imagine he prayed something like, "God, help me know what to do," like this would do any good. I promised not to tell any of his friends.

For a week he said, "One day I want to play school ball, and the next day I want competitive ball. I can't make up my mind."

I don't think I had ever discussed seeking God's direction through prayer with my son. Gideon went to church because of his family and friends. Following Jesus didn't cross his mind. He would take his turn sometimes praying before meals, always starting with, "Thank you, dear God, for this wonderful day you have given us," followed by "Thanks for the food, Amen." It might have been the only prayer he ever prayed.

It was unusual for him to confide in me with a problem and ask for advice. So I told him what I would do in his situation, and he was willing to try it, being out of other ideas. I was careful not to give him a specific line to say, so he would pray in his own words.

Two things were bothering Gideon that made him try prayer. First, he wanted two things very important to him, and he couldn't have both at the same time. Second, there was an internal daily tug-of-war inside him – a pendulum that swung one way, then the other, back and forth. He couldn't put the decision off, due to a deadline. He asked God what to do as a desperate last-choice solution.

How did God make the right choice clear to my son?

He asked God to give him guidance, and he was willing to listen, even though the only way he could imagine God talking to someone was through an audible voice, like how Charlton Heston heard God say, "Moses!" in *The Ten Commandments*. We want God to let us know in a real and tangible way. We want God to shout, when often God whispers.

The day before the deadline, Gideon came to me with light in his eyes. He said, "I know what to do! I'm going with school ball. I woke up this morning and the conflict was gone!" To his utter shock, asking God for direction worked. Gideon asked because time was short, and this was a really important decision. He chose to engage God because it was deeply important in his life.

How did God answer his prayer? Did he hear God speak aloud from heaven? No, the internal conflict disappeared, leaving one desire instead of two.

How did he know the answer came from God? The conflict hadn't gone away through any other means. Could he explain it? No. Gideon knew what to do now, because choice was no longer an issue. He didn't have to choose, because there was only one answer – kind of like voting when there's only one candidate.

God had replaced conflict with peace.

> *God is not a God of confusion but of peace. 1 Corinthians 14:33 (NASB)*

One of the ways I know God is speaking to me is when something happens that meets an immediate need through an unexpected source.

Once when I was going through a particularly difficult time, I felt like a total failure. I had screwed up again and again, and came to believe the lie that I was hopeless.

I usually listen to a Christian radio station in my car. That day I had to run an errand. When I started my car, a song was playing on the radio, beginning at the very first verse.

The song said everyone fails sometimes and feels the pain is more than we can stand. It said I was stronger than I knew. Believing something was impossible wasn't a reason to give up, because God was going to heal my broken heart. God would remove this mountain, no matter how I felt, and He could help me find my way out of this mess if I trusted Him. God promised me that things were going to change for the better.

That song gave me hope, and God had it played just for me, so I could hear His message of love and forgiveness. There is no way that event happened by chance or fate. God caused it to happen so I would know He was speaking to me.

God wants us to know that we know that we know we're hearing from Him, and He'll make sure of it, if we are willing to listen.

This is what Uncensored Prayer is all about. It's about learning to listen and hear from God. We can ask God about anything, big or little. Nothing is too trivial or far-fetched. It delights God every time we come to Him, regardless about how we feel and what we want to talk about. Isn't that wonderful?

God Reveals Things We Don't Know.

Throughout Scripture, God consistently speaks to people telling them things they didn't know. In other words, God will confirm it's Him by making us aware of things we *couldn't* already know.

> *Call to Me and I will answer you, and I will tell you great and mighty things, which you do not know. Jeremiah 33:3 (NASB)*

From now on I will tell you of new things, of hidden things unknown to you. Isaiah 48:6 (NIV)

It seems strange that God would work this way. We're not prophets seeking to gain fortune in the next big lottery. We're not trying to take advantage of God with inside information. Yet God chooses to give us what we don't know as a way of confirming it's from Him.

When I was 28 years old, shortly after surgery, I lost my job and most everything I had. About all I could pray was, "God, *now* what am I going to do?" My parents invited me to come live with them until I could get a job and find a place to live.

I moved in with them right before Thanksgiving. One day, my parents and I were sitting in their kitchen when the phone rang. Daddy answered it and listened for a few minutes. Then he held the phone away from his ear, looked at me and said, "Want to buy a house?" Before I could answer, he put the phone back to his ear and said, "We'll take it!"

The lady across the street had just reconciled with her husband, who lived hundreds of miles away. She wanted to move back there in time to get her kids in school when spring term started the beginning of January – six weeks from then. She had an assumable V.A. loan with the bank for half the house's value, and was willing to finance the remaining money personally. I had no job, no money, and no credit. How on earth was I going to buy a house?

Daddy offered to co-sign the mortgage with me, and make the payments to the bank and the home owner until I had a job and could pay them on my own. And that's exactly what occurred.

No one knew any of this was going to happen. I didn't know I was going to lose my job and needed a place to go. The neighbor didn't know she would reconcile with her husband and need to sell her house ASAP. I didn't know I was suddenly going to own a house, having no job, money or credit.

What happened here? God answered my simple prayer of "God, *now* what am I going to do?" for both the neighbor and me in an extraordinary way, revealing solutions we didn't know were possible. Obviously, this was an astonishing act of God.

When I spend time alone wrestling with God, I also learn new things about Him and myself that I have never considered before. Sometimes I can't understand these unfamiliar ideas or they seem like total lunacy to me. God says, "You betcha!"

> *For My thoughts are not your thoughts, neither are your ways My ways, says the Lord.*
>
> *For as the heavens are higher than the earth, so are My ways higher than your ways and My thoughts than your thoughts.*
> *Isaiah 55:8-9 (AMP)*

So why would God bother telling me His thoughts? Well, for one thing, to prove He's a lot smarter that me (no questions there). But also so God can interpret what He wants me to know in a way I can understand.

Jesus did this all the time when he told parables to the crowds. Some people got the point, but others didn't, including the disciples many times. That's why Jesus pulled his team aside and explained what his story meant. These were men who had chosen to follow him, so Jesus taught them spiritual truths that a mixed crowd of believers and skeptics weren't ready to hear. Jesus spent time teaching his crew, because they were going to explain these truths to other people once Jesus was gone.

Confirmation From Scripture

Hearing from God also begins with Scripture. When we really need to know if God is talking with us, we can go straight to Scripture to confirm it. Have you ever been reading a passage in the Bible you've read many times before, and suddenly a verse jumps off the page with pointblank relevancy? What's happening here? The words suddenly apply to your current situation, answering a troubling question.

> *All Scripture is inspired by God and is useful to teach us what is true and to make us realize what is wrong in our lives. It corrects us when we are wrong and teaches us to do what is right. 2 Timothy 3:16 (NLT)*

The beautiful part about Scripture is that if we're willing to listen, it will always speak to us in just the right way. If we're willing to search the Scriptures, we will find the right words that will speak to us.

Just the other day, God and I had been wrestling through Uncensored Prayer about my career as an author, trusting God to take care of bills, and me worrying about it. I knew I had heard God promise to take care of all my concerns on this topic. But internally I was struggling to see how it was possible. My fears were getting the best of me.

So I pulled out my Bible and just started reading. I'm a cross referencing junkie when I study my Bible, and many times the answer to a concern God and I have been wrestling about shows up in a cross reference – somewhere I wasn't even looking. I started reading in Isaiah, and a verse cross referenced to a verse in Proverbs:

> *A man will be satisfied with good by the fruit of his words,*
> *And the deeds of a man's hands will return to him.*
> *Proverbs 12:14 (NASB)*

That verse cross referenced to another verse:

> *With the fruit of a man's mouth his stomach will be satisfied;*
> *He will be satisfied with the product of his lips. Proverbs*
> *18:20 (NASB)*

Suddenly I was aware of what I had always known: God would take care of my needs. The verse hadn't given me anything new. It had reiterated what I had forgotten. The words had settled my heart. God had spoken directly to me through His Word.

Scripture is valuable because it consistently reminds us that God cares. It's a vast source of wisdom for how God consistently loves us. In moments of trouble, God gives us just what we need, not just in tangible things, but also peace about our worries and concerns.

Confirmation From Others

In learning to hear from God, it is also important to remember that God also speaks to us through friends. Sometimes we just need to ask a wise friend for counsel, and God can speak to us through them.

The way of a fool is right in his own eyes, but he who listens to counsel is wise. Proverbs 12:15 (AMP)

Wisdom is found in those who take advice. Proverbs 13:10 (NIV)

When I first got sober, my sponsor told me to call her everyday. One morning I got up shaking so badly, I knew I couldn't go to work, so I called her. She said, "So, can you take a shower?" "Of course I can take a shower!" I quavered. "Go take a shower and call me back." Then she hung up.

After my shower, I called her back, and told her I couldn't face work that day. "Well, can you get dressed?" she said. Now she was starting to piss me off. "Of course I can get dressed!" I said angrily. "Get dressed, then call me." And she slammed the phone down.

Cursing under my breath, I got dressed and called her. "Are you dressed?" she asked. I replied, "Yes. Stop the stupid questions, because I need to talk to you." "Call me when you get to work, then we'll talk." I slammed down the phone, and headed to my car. "I'll show you I can get to work, you old blank-blank-blank."

When I sat down at my desk, I called her with shaking hands, saying, "I'm here, but I can't function. Are you happy now?" She said, "What's the first thing you see in front of you?" I looked down at my desk and replied, "The mail." "Well, open your mail and call me back."

That's how she got me through that day. I couldn't pray right then, but she was praying for me by what she did. Later she told me she called this process "The Next Indicated Thing." Whenever I felt overwhelmed or panicky, I needed to pause and ask God, "What's the next indicated thing to do?"

My sponsor said this was a prayer God would answer every time, immediately. I would see a simple task right in front of me, like opening the mail or taking a shower. Then my job was to do it. God would show me an easy task I could do – not busy work, but something that needed doing. Focusing on one uncomplicated chore took my mind off of feeling overwhelmed, and calmed me down. It works. I highly recommend trying it.

Asking "What's the next indicated thing to do?" was one of the first ways I heard God answer me directly. I knew it was an answer to my prayer, because one minute I was so overwhelmed I had ceased functioning effectively. There was too much to do in too little time, and I had too little brain left to deal with it. Then I prayed and saw, right in front of me, something I was capable of doing that needed to be done that day. I felt like God was saying,

> *Do this task for the moment and calm down, then I'll help you sort out what's on fire and must be done today, and what can wait until later.*

Doing something was much more effective than doing nothing and stewing over it. I needed constructive action, not scattered, hurricane action that only left a splintered day and mind in its wake. God knew exactly what I needed, and gave it when I cried out for help. And it came in the form of a trusted friend.

Asking for the next indicated thing to do is one of the most practical and effective prayers I've ever learned to say when I feel stressed. And a friend taught me how to do it by pissing me off.

God is willing to speak if we are willing to listen. God will reveal things we didn't know to let us know it's from Him. And when we're just not sure, we can search out the Scriptures or ask a trusted friend.

If you're like me, there's always that little voice in the back of your mind saying, "What if I'm wrong? These are deeply important matters." Yet one thing is certain. If you don't try, you'll never know. The mystery can only be resolved by trying, by stepping onto the mat with God and trusting.

As you read this book, I invite you to pushback. I welcome you to disagree with me and question what I say. I ask myself frequently, when I think I've heard from God, "What if I'm just telling myself what I want to hear, or am I replaying old tapes from my past?" I have no easy answers for those questions. But I feel freedom to question God and disagree with Him, which I used to believe was blasphemy. Now I recognize that most of my fears are really about how afraid I am of being honest with myself.

During these intimate conversations with God, I sense we're in sacred space, no matter where we are. I have no desire for you to just automatically take my word for this, and I will never assert that Uncensored Prayer is right for you. But I will offer what I've learned in my own journey with God, and the path I'm taking. I invite you to try unlicensed, unlimited honesty with God.

Chapter 2

Learning From Jacob

The idea of wrestling is not a little idea in the story in Scripture. The nation of Israel is named after "the one who wrestles". The very essence of the Jewish identity was found in the moment of great risk. Jacob was Abraham's grandson. And although Abraham was the founder of the Jewish faith, the Israelite nation got its name and true character through Jacob.

Jacob wasn't like his granddad. Where Abraham succeeded in faith, Jacob failed miserably. He was a scoundrel, a liar, and a thief. But instead of wallowing in his failure, he took the risk to confront his personal issues and had a life-changing experience with God.

And Jacob was left alone, and a Man wrestled with him until daybreak.

And when [the Man] saw that He did not prevail against [Jacob], He touched the hollow of his thigh; and Jacob's thigh was put out of joint as he wrestled with Him.

Then He said, Let Me go, for day is breaking. But [Jacob] said, I will not let You go unless You declare a blessing upon me.

[The Man] asked him, What is your name? And [in shock of realization, whispering] he said, Jacob [supplanter, schemer, trickster, swindler]!

> *And He said, Your name shall be called no more Jacob [supplanter], but Israel [contender with God]; for you have contended and have power with God and with men and have prevailed. Genesis 32:24-28 (AMP)*

Jacob took the risk to wrestle and helped change the face of a nation. The identity of Israel came out of *Jacob's* experience of wrestling. It came after years of running from the truth and finally taking the risk to face it.

Jacob showed a great deal of faith by wrestling with God and refusing to stop without a blessing. Abraham and Jacob's faith were different and personal. God honors our Bank of Faith debit card, no matter how little faith we have, because He's the one who gives us the amount we need to believe in Him.

The story of Jacob wrestling offers six lessons: *Get alone with God, take the initiative, wrestling with God is often painful, ask for what you want, your perspective about yourself will change, and your perspective about God will change.*

Get Alone With God

Jacob and his family had been living with Jacob's father-in-law, Laban, for many years. The time came in God's plan for Jacob to come back home.

> *Then the Lord said to Jacob, Return to the land of your fathers and to your people, and I will be with you. Genesis 31:3 (AMP)*

Yet coming home meant facing the truth. Jacob had used fraud and deception to steal his brother Esau's birthright and his father's blessing, Esau's right as the firstborn son. The last time the brothers had been together, Esau vowed to kill Jacob.

By following God's instruction to return to the land of his people, Jacob knew there was a real possibility he would die if he ever met Esau again. So in following God's directive, Jacob was taking a real risk that things would work out.

Sure enough, Esau learned that Jacob was headed his way, and when Jacob found out, he was seriously frightened. Then he received the lovely news

Learning From Jacob

that Esau had 400 men with him, while Jacob had his wives, children, and the rest of his household. Not exactly equal odds for what might be a very nasty confrontation.

It's easy to imagine that Jacob had no idea how to handle this dilemma. His fear was obvious. But he still took the risk because restoration was not possible without it. So Jacob sent his family on ahead, and spent a sleepless night wrestling. And the rest they say is history.

Wrestling with God often begins with creating a space to just be alone. Jesus knew the importance of spending time alone with his Father, especially after a long day of miracles, helping people, and teaching disciples who could be soooo dense (Sound familiar? I can be like that).

> *After He had sent the crowds away, He went up on the mountain by Himself to pray; and when it was evening, He was there alone. Matthew 14:23 (NASB)*

Practicing Uncensored Prayer requires private time with God.

> *But when you pray, go away by yourself, shut the door behind you, and pray to your Father in private. Then your Father, who sees everything, will reward you. Matthew 6:6 (NLT)*

As an author, I can't write with people around or background noise like the TV. Distractions and interruptions get in the way of hearing God and my own heart. The same principle applies to Uncensored Prayer. Even if you talk to God out loud, you need a private place to do it, where no one but God will hear, allowing your heart freedom to be honest.

Don't cheat yourself by making a 10-minute appointment with God, like it was a parent/teacher conference at elementary school. You might have only 30 minutes to spend with Him, or the best opportunity you have to get alone with God is early in the morning before anyone else gets up. God doesn't give stars on your report card for perfect daily attendance. Just make private time with God a priority as you can, when you need it.

Finding time alone gives us the space to remove all the obstacles that keep us from hearing directly from God. Sometimes I don't *want* time alone with God when I'm pretty sure He's got a message for me I don't want to hear about something I'm not willing to face or refuse to do. Trying to avoid God doesn't work, because He won't leave. But He might just remain silent when we refuse to listen.

Before Jacob returned to the land of his fathers, he had been running. He was avoiding the truth. He was avoiding God. Wrestling with God means refusing to run. I've avoided God so many times I can't begin to count them. I've made unwise decisions and acted on them, not wanting unpleasant consequences, yet doing it anyway because I wanted what I wanted.

For Jacob to return he had to confront his issues. Getting on the wrestling mat first requires dealing with the mess we made. It requires admitting it to ourselves. God already knows what we've done. In all cases, honesty and humility are necessary but not easy.

Yet in taking the risk to confront the issue Jacob discovered restoration. In returning he was able to reconcile and discover his brother had forgiven him.

I'm going to be bold enough to say you need time alone with God. And God wants time alone with you.

Take The Initiative

Engaging in Uncensored Prayer requires taking the initiative with God. God is already waiting to talk with us, but we have to be willing to seek Him. There are a lot more instances in the Bible of people praying than God showing up to make an announcement.

In Genesis 32, God invites Jacob home, but Jacob took the initiative to go home. He created the space to wrestle all night with God.

God will not invade our lives. God will not force us to wrestle with Him. It's one thing to know we want or need to struggle through something with God, but action on our part is required. Faith is taking the initiative, believing that such a confrontation will actually mean something. God is always in the process of drawing everyone to Him, even those who don't believe He exists. For those of us who already believe, God yanks at the cord.

Compared to his grandfather, Abraham, Jacob had very little experience with exercising faith, mainly because he didn't use it. Maybe he thought he didn't

Learning From Jacob

have any. Jacob was very self-centered, taking what he wanted without asking. So what prompted him to take the initiative and head off for the land of his fathers? I think it was time. It took what it took up to now in Jacob's life for him to be ready to listen to God, and a willingness to listen goes hand in hand with a willingness to follow God's advice.

The Bible doesn't tell us what finally made Jacob ready to follow God's directive and leave town, headed for his own personal Promised Land. Something happened. For Jacob, leaving town was Step One in his new relationship with God. Step Two was recognizing his need to talk with God. Step Three was initiating his wrestling match with God, and something HUGE happened that changed Jacob's entire life this time.

I've been writing poetry most of my life, and the only person I've had to please was me. Last year other people were pleased enough with my work to talk me into writing this book, which both delights me and scares the crap out of me because it's unknown territory.

As I was writing this book I encountered a significant tension with the process of writing. I needed to use a new program to write but I couldn't figure it out. God had called me to write professionally and my editor has made that possible – both miracles I couldn't do by myself, enabling my heart's desire to come true.

I was mad at God for placing me in a position I thought I couldn't handle. I was mad at my editor for asking me to learn something new and making me feel stupid. I felt like I was the problem child, even though I wasn't trying to be. I was embarrassed and didn't know what to do.

So I took the initiative to take on God in a wrestling match. We fought as many rounds as I needed to vent and cry and scream. I dumped all my frustration and fear on God. He assured me everything was going to be OK, and I mentally believed Him, even though my emotions hadn't changed. I knew from previous experience the emotion part would come – sometime.

Wrestling with God in Uncensored Prayer hasn't made everything all better, except in one crucial way: I have somewhere to go, someone to tell who I know I can't offend, who understands my pain and anger. I know by experience I have nothing to fear about my relationship being damaged with Him.

How do we learn that initiating wrestling with God is safe? How can we learn that God won't get mad at us for being mad at Him? Initiative. Risk. Trust. And wrestling.

I first initiated wrestling with God through Uncensored Prayer because I believed He was already mad at me, so I had nothing to lose. I wanted to beat God up until He hurt as badly as I hurt. I needed to vent my rage and pain no matter what the consequences would be. Risk didn't matter anymore – I was that mad.

God wasn't surprised He had it coming, but He sure as hell surprised me by screaming back at me, not out of anger, but out of love. I had been so hurt and mad that I had lost the capacity to hear His life-long whispers of love, so screaming at me was as necessary for God as it was necessary for me.

I had to do something different so God could do something different in our relationship. I had to go to Him for me to really hear Him for the first time. Little did I know we had had a relationship all along, though the love and trust part was one-sided on God's side of the fence. The relationship was already there. He was already my Daddy. He was with me all the time, preventing some disasters from happening and helping me through others. It wasn't until much later that I was able to look back on my life and see evidence of what He'd done for me all along.

Many of us have heard that God's salvation is a free gift, but it doesn't make any difference to us personally until we take it, receive it, and open it. God's been saving us from the beginning, but our relationship with Him changes when we take the initiative to have a personal relationship with God, so that it's give and take, not just God giving.

We don't have to get mad at God to begin having a deeper relationship with Him through Uncensored Prayer. We just have to take the initiative out of curiosity, faith, doubt, or fear. And even anger. It doesn't matter *why*, but it does matter that we *do*.

My story is my example, and I encourage you to take the initiative to struggle with God. The worst that can happen is God will bite your head off, and then you can tell your friends that God really is terrifying and whatever you do, don't listen to the nut who wrote this book.

But what if I'm right? What if Jacob was right? What if Jesus was right? Remember, Jesus took the initiative to come to earth looking for us, bringing forgiveness and freedom for all the world. Are you willing to take the initiative to go looking for him?

> *"For the Son of Man came to seek and save those who are lost."* John 19:10 (NLT)

We're all lost, but we have to be willing to be found. In God's humanly illogical world, we have to go to Him to be found. Are you willing to take the initiative to go looking for Him? The only thing you have to lose is fear, regret, frustration and isolation.

Wrestling With God Is Often Painful

When we engage with God in Uncensored Prayer, getting on the mat and wrestling through our fears and doubts, it often results in pain. Jacob was wounded in his wrestling match, but he wouldn't let go until he got what he wanted. He didn't want a trophy. He wanted a blessing, and God honored that request. God rewarded Jacob for his willingness and initiative. His prize was huge: a new name and identity, plus power with God and people. But the cost of wrestling with God was a receiving limp – a physical injury that would remain.

> *This left Jacob all alone in the camp, and a man came and wrestled with him until the dawn began to break. When the man saw that he would not win the match, he touched Jacob's hip and wrenched it out of its socket.*
>
> *The sun was rising when Jacob left Peniel, and he was limping because of the injury to his hip.* Genesis 32:24, 25, 31 (NLV)

When we engage in Uncensored Prayer, it often involves stark honesty about ourselves and how we feel, and that often hurts. None of us like admitting unflattering truth about ourselves, even to God, who already knows. I think the pain actually comes from facing the truth about ourselves, that we're not perfect. How could God love us if we're not? And when we hold onto this lie it causes us so much shame and fear about our total inadequacy to change or handle so many situations. Hebrews 12:1 calls it, *"the sin that so easily entangles" (NIV)*. It's the fear that there is actually something we can do to lose the love of God.

God uses the pain for our redemption, to release us from the ties that bind us. When we step onto the wrestling mat, we are often left with the painful reminders of our choices we have made to hide from God, or ignore our past. But it is only when we confront our past, which is painful, that we can begin to engage in our own restoration.

Jesus wasn't afraid of pain. In fact, he ran towards it. The wounds of Jesus were necessary for our healing and peace.

> *But He was wounded for our transgressions, He was bruised for our guilt and iniquities; the chastisement [needful to obtain] peace and well-being for us was upon Him, and with the stripes [that wounded] Him we are healed and made whole. Isaiah 53:5 (AMP)*

I have wrestled with God due to pain, which caused additional pain by facing truth that hurt. But the payoff has been relief from having to bear that burden alone, and peace that comes from experiencing God's forgiveness and compassion. From that, I have gained courage and strength to face times of pain in my life, knowing God understands and is there for me.

I spent a couple of months on short-term disability from a debilitating disease until it became evident that I could no longer work outside my home for an indeterminate period of time, perhaps years. Unforeseen blessings came out of this situation. I was able to write, and focus full time on being an author. It opened up my heart to what I've wanted to do for a long time.

When a personal disaster occurs, like severe illness, losing a job or our mate, it's hard to see any good happening at all. Catastrophic disasters, like war or when whole communities are wiped out by a terrible storm, can make us wonder why a loving God allows such human suffering. Having faith in

God's providence at such moments can be very difficult to maintain, or even have at all.

The loss of my job meant a loss of finances, which created a new fear. But in the midst of this fear God provided in ways that I least expected. But my fear became the space for me to cry out to God. It became a reminder that I needed Him.

Paul wrote,

> *God causes all things to work together for good to those who love God, to those who are called according to His purpose.*
> *Romans 8:28 (NASB)*

Pain is not fun, but it reminds us of our need for God. Without pain there is no need for healing. If we feel sufficient to handle our own difficulties, there is no need for God.

> *Therefore, since we are surrounded by such a great cloud of witnesses, let us throw off everything that hinders and the sin that so easily entangles. And let us run with perseverance the race marked out for us, fixing our eyes on Jesus, the pioneer and perfecter of faith. For the joy set before him he endured the cross, scorning its shame, and sat down at the right hand of the throne of God. Consider him who endured such opposition from sinners, so that you will not grow weary and lose heart. Hebrews 12:1-3 (NIV)*

Yes, you might find wrestling with God is painful. It hurts and is never easy when we talk with God about personal shame and being disappointed with ourself. But like Jacob, God has a custom-made blessing for those who wrestle with Him.

Do you want your blessing?

Ask For What You Want

I have no doubt that Jacob wrestled out of fear. In returning to the land of his fathers, he had to confront his past. And his brother could have easily killed him. In fact it was likely, given their history. But there was something Jacob wanted badly enough to fight for, and he refused to end the fight until he received a blessing. In other words, Jacob asked for what he really wanted.

Jacob had his father's blessing, but it was Esau's by right, and Jacob took it away from his brother by fraud. Isaac had a blessing with Jacob's name on it, but he never got it because he was greedy. Jacob had finally come to a place in his life where he wanted his *own* personal blessing, – one that wasn't stolen. This was the blessing God had saved for Jacob from birth, but Jacob had to ask for it.

I ended up at my first 12 Step meeting for alcoholics through the back door. A friend of mine kept giving me a hard time about my drinking and driving while in a blackout, and the trouble it was causing in my life. So I went to this meeting to get her off my case, figuring a bunch of drunks could tell me how to drink and drive successfully.

I didn't get what I came for. These people were dangerously insane. They revealed their worst secrets and behavior, something I went to great lengths to lie about and hide (little did I know how much people in my life knew about me). Truth was the enemy, alcohol was my friend, and a person did what they had to do to protect themselves, right? Yes, drinking like I did had some annoying consequences, but I didn't want to stop badly enough to quit.

But there was another shocker at the meeting that scared me. Many of these people looked at me with a deep sense of understanding and compassion that was as foreign to me as aliens. And they claimed they got their peace because they followed a simple set of suggestions called the 12 Steps.

But I didn't have to worry about that ridiculous list. A passage from their literature was read aloud that disqualified me from this program: God could and would help me with my drinking problem if I simply asked him. What a relief. I didn't belong here. Sure, God helped some people, but He didn't help me. I had a life-time of proof. God *could* but He *wouldn't* for me. I could envision Him looking at me and shrugging His shoulders and saying, "Sorry. Next in line, please?"

But the compassionate eyes I saw at that meeting haunted me, and a deep ache rose up in my heart that wouldn't go away. I wasn't ready to stop drinking, but I longed for the peace they had. I was tired of lying and hiding, and it troubled me that it no longer caused them shame, because something had delivered them and they said it was God.

I was now miserable and it was their fault. Those people had something I desperately wanted but couldn't have, which compelled me to go back to those meetings. Against my better judgment I couldn't stay away.

One horrific day of drinking, I was able to admit to myself that alcohol was ruining my life, and I wanted help. I went to a meeting and asked for their help and they surrounded me with their love and promises of support.

Then a very unexpected thing happened. I went home, got on my knees by my bed, and prayed a one-liner to God: "God, I know you *could*, but I'm asking you to *would* for me." That was it. No angels sang, and I didn't feel a bit different. So I just went to bed.

When I got up the next morning and looked in the mirror, I saw peaceful, unprotected eyes looking back at me, and I knew a miracle had happened. God had given me what I asked for.

Somehow I don't believe God would have granted my request before that day, not just because I hadn't asked. I hadn't believed. Not one bit. But like Jacob, the day came where I wanted my *own* blessing, and I wanted it badly enough to ask for it.

What do you really wish you could ask God? I mean *really*. Now ask yourself, "What am I afraid of?" That's the issue, isn't it? We're afraid of God's wrath, disapproval, blame. Who told us that? God? Other people, right? If we believe that a God of "love" is really a God of wrath, that's a good reason not to want to spend time with Him. Like I used to, you might think truth is the enemy. Well, it certainly *is* dangerous to tell some people the truth. Self-preservation is a human instinct. Putting ourselves in harm's way isn't.

Would it scare you to death to find out God is filled with compassion and unconditional love? Why would good things like that scare us? Perhaps because it would be a serious paradigm shift in how we view God. Perhaps you think, like I did, that God might accept and help other people, but not me, because I've (fill-in-the blank) or have done (fill-in-the blank).

Fear of God typically keeps us from relating with Him. It keeps us from Uncensored Prayer. It keeps us from asking because we assume God doesn't want us. We believe the lie that God could never, ever handle our honest dialogue, or would never give us good gifts. It's so much safer to do what we've taught rather than explore new things for ourselves. "If it ain't broke, don't fix it." Don't rock the boat. Don't go looking for what we probably can't have.

Often during financially lean times in my life, I've refused to go window-shopping at the mall with friends, because why see something I wish I could have but can't. That would only reinforce the feelings of inadequacy because I was broke. But what if the only one keeping me spiritually and emotionally broke is me?

Everybody has a direct line to God. *Anyone* can have a deeply intimate relationship with Him. Every person has an invitation from God for unlimited one-on-one time with Him, and He longs for honest, uncensored conversations with all of us (if you think that doesn't include you, I hate to tell you, but you're not that special. Sorry).

Jesus even instructs us to ask.

> *Ask, and it will be given to you; seek, and you will find; knock, and it will be opened to you.* Matthew 7:7 (NASB)

I encourage you today to ask God for what you want. Keep on asking until you know His answer (refer to Chapter One for a refresher course, if needed). At the heart of our pain is the same thing Jacob wanted. We want to know God loves us.

If you don't like His answer, tell Him it's my fault for talking you into this.

Your Perspective About Yourself Will Change

It's very common in some cultures to give children names according to what they mean, and that name can be changed later in life based on a significant event or personal achievement. I deliberately named my children for characteristics I claimed for them.

My daughter's name is *Grace Katharine Joy*, which means: *Unmerited Favor*

Learning From Jacob

of God, Pure and Joyful. My oldest son's name is *Gideon James*, which means: *Mighty Warrior and Supplanter*. My youngest son's name is *Gabriel Jeremiah*, which means: *A Man of God Whom the Lord Honors*.

Gideon's middle name, James, is a form of Jacob (no, I didn't choose the primary Bible story in this book in honor of my son. Sorry, Gideon). My daddy's name is James, and he's one of the godliest men I know, with characteristics I claim for my son. My prayer is my children's names will become their identities.

Jacob's name had become his identity, but it wasn't good. He perceived himself as a schemer, trickster, swindler, and so lived that way. But that's not how God saw him. Once Jacob was honest with himself, God changed his name to Israel, which means *"contender with God" Genesis 32:28 (AMP)*. Other translations say, *"struggles with God" (NIV)* and *"fights with God" (NLT)*.

Jacob didn't view himself as a good guy. Sure, he had street smarts, but not integrity. A transformational relationship with God was not on Jacob's agenda. But he *had* sought out God for this confrontation. Jacob needed to release his pent up fear and perhaps anger. But he also wanted God's blessing, and refused to quit fighting until he got it.

Do you know what God gave him? Responsibility. Yippee. God gave Jacob virtually the same blessing Abraham had received: to be blessed and to be a blessing. He would now be the leader of a nation, God's chosen people. That mantle of leadership passed from Abraham to Isaac, and from Isaac to Jacob. I don't know if Jacob had ever thought of himself as a leader. But now God said, "Surprise! You've just been commissioned as a leader of a nation."

It's easy to envision Jacob thinking, "I don't know how to be a leader, or what to do. Now what?" Once Jacob bought into the vision, his perspective about himself changed. God's affirmation that Jacob was now a leader enabled Jacob to see himself as a leader. He started acting like a leader, and he followed God's leadership.

Wrestling with God becomes the space to trade in the lie that we are not worth it. We're all seeking God's blessing, and when we embrace God's love our perspective changes. When I followed God's direction to write and publish this book, I had no idea what I was getting myself into. Family members and good friends started sharing their beliefs that God would bless this book, leading to other books and speaking engagements. It's scary when you hear the same thing from individuals who haven't talked with each other. I hadn't bargained for such a huge plan. I wasn't qualified to do this.

Through the vision of these people whom I trust and know to be close to God, I began taking my fears and feelings to God in Uncensored Prayer. With His help, my perspective about myself has begun to change. It still seems farfetched, but I *can* follow God into the vast unknown of His call for me. He will enable me to meet each challenge as they arrive and not before.

My responsibility today is to simply be who I am, and follow God's instructions for today only. See, I had thought God was asking me to instantly transform into someone completely different than I am right now. But that's not how God works. He has shared his vision for my life, and asked me to be willing to move that direction with Him.

Everything God asks us to do today is something within our current ability, and with His power, He enables us to do just that, with results greater than we can achieve on own. I call that a miracle. It's easy to see the miracle of God's creation every time we walk outside or look at a newborn baby. We are all miracles of God's handiwork, but God is also constantly causing personal miracles to happen for each of us.

The more we engage in the spiritual practice of wrestling with God, and become willing to listen to Him, He is able to do so much more in and through us. And God doesn't just color outside the box. He doesn't have any boxes. There are no limits to God's love.

> *He causes his sun to rise on the evil and the good, and sends rain on the righteous and the unrighteous. Matthew 5:45 (NIV)*

We are each unique yet ordinary children of God. We're all a lot like Jacob. He was just a regular person. We are "equal opportunity" members of God's family. God blesses everyone but some just realize it more than others. Jacob just took the risk to ask for it. He had it comin'. I can hear God saying, *"You want to be blessed? You got it. Surprise!"*

Have you noticed how many Biblical "heroes" were just average people through whom God did extraordinary things? David, Peter, Jesus' mother Mary. As different as these individuals were, they all had some key similarities: they were willing to wrestle with God through Uncensored Prayer. They were willing to follow God into His amazing plan for their lives, which required allowing faith to supersede logic. And they were teachable, keeping an open mind and heart for God's revelations and truth.

When we seek God's blessing, we discover a unique calling, a mission that is custom-designed. You may already be aware of God's heartsong within you. If not, spend more and more time with God. You might as well prepare yourself for a shock. The day will come when God reveals His plan for your life, and it will change your perspective about yourself. It's also not a once-in-a-lifetime experience. Traveling with God is always an adventure, leading to new revelations.

Every time it happens to me, I go into temporary cardiac arrest. Then I discover God's itinerary for me is amazing. A true miracle.

Go ask God for your own miracle. At the right time, He'll say, "Surprise!"

Your Perspective About God Will Change

When Jacob wrestled, a strange thing happened. First he received a new name. But the second was even more shocking: he received power.

> *And He said, Your name shall be called no more Jacob [supplanter], but Israel [contender with God]; for you have contended and have power with God and with men and have prevailed. Genesis 32:28 (AMP)*

What? It's easy to read that and assume it says, "You can have power over God." But that's not what it says. When we wrestle with God we discover how powerful we actually are. Wrestling with God gives us power *with* God, because we're in relationship with the One who is powerful. Genesis 32:28 says, "*You have struggled with God and with humans and **have overcome**"* (NIV). Another says, "*You have fought with God and with men and **have won**"* (NLT).

Without relationship, we don't have the power to overcome our fears, hurts, and every hindrance that keeps us from being who God made us to be. But with God, we have the power to prevail, to overcome the lies that oppress us. And when we prevail, our perspective of God changes. God is not on the other side. We're now on God's side.

Do you think what God said to Jacob changed his perspective about his heavenly Father? I have no doubt about it. What God told Jacob must have shocked him. It certainly shocks me. I imagine this was so upside-down and backwards from Jacob's perception of God and himself that he had to think long and hard about it, and it must have taken quite awhile for Jacob to take it all in. I bet Jacob and God had some *really* interesting conversations on this topic.

I don't know if Jacob had ever wrestled with God before this time. His experience with Uncensored Prayer may have been similar to mine when I first started praying like this. I was too hurt to care if what I said to God was appropriate or not. Words and feelings just poured out of me.

Some of my perspective of God changed immediately. For starters, I wasn't struck by lightning (Don't laugh. It seemed like a reasonable possibility at the time). Second, I sensed somehow that God really was listening and wasn't mad at me. I don't know how I knew that, but I just did. I think God made sure I knew. Over time, my perspective about God has dramatically changed since I started the spiritual practice of wrestling with Him through Uncensored Prayer. When I could see that God actually loved me for who I am, and not just who I thought I should be, it changed everything. It gave me a desire to help others know His love. My heart poured out for those who were on the outside looking in.

Sometimes new insights about God come to us gently. Sometimes it's a massive explosion. However it comes, God seriously wants us to know Him better, and will reveal Himself to us when He thinks best. For God to be able to do that, we have to be willing to learn.

Do you have an open mind for God to reveal Himself to you in some unexpected ways? You may find yourself astounded at how much God loves you. He might clarify some misconceptions you have about Him. He might implode one of your most rock-solid beliefs. Think about the culture crisis the disciples had when they found Jesus talking with the Samaritan woman at the well. How might that have rearranged their beliefs about God?

Spending intimate time alone with God will change you. Engaging in the spiritual practice of wrestling with God will alter some of your beliefs and strengthen others, and you alone can decide if any of this will happen. You have to be willing. Are you?

One of the joys of uncensored time with God is discovering new things about Him, many of which replace things we previously believed. We each have a defined image of God based on what we've been taught and our life experiences. But if that image of God doesn't look like Jesus, it's false. So when Jesus was willing to touch the leper, and heal the blind man, he wasn't just performing miracles. He was redefining our perception of how God relates to the least of these.

The reason Jesus made the Pharisees so mad was he claimed to be God, challenged their teachings, and uncovered their hypocrisy. They knew they were "right" and he wasn't. I would like to take things one-step further. I suggest that if God the Father had stood before them making the exact same statements, and they *knew* it was God the Father, the Pharisees wouldn't have believed they were wrong.

For the Pharisees, being "right" was more important than being right. They were unwilling to have a genuine encounter with God that would change their perspectives about Him or themselves. They weren't teachable, so Jesus said,

> *Your choice. Now please get out of my way so I can help some people with an open mind.*

God is infinitely more than we can comprehend, and infinitely is probably too small a word. Engaging with God in Uncensored Prayer is the space to rediscover a God that looks like Jesus. Jacob discovered this. Jesus discovered this. And we can too.

Chapter 3

What We Gain By Wrestling With God

When we wrestle with God through Uncensored Prayer, we learn that God is already willing to give us the best. And sometimes it feels strange to think that God wants to give us the best. It's easy to think that we're supposed to settle for less, or just enough. But Jacob was given a rich blessing, one that would eventually help transform the world.

In the absence of God's best, we often strive to get the next best thing. It's easy to covet something we want, feeling like, "What's mine is mine, and what's yours should be mine, too." We gravitate towards stuff because it's tangible. We think it can take away our hidden pain or make us feel adequate. We hold on tightly because we're afraid of losing it. To wrestle with God is to discover the rich blessing that can never be taken away.

Wanting the best isn't always about greed or status. Jesus came to give us abundant life. To live life to the fullest, rich in love and peace is what God wants for us. Achieving those goals is a difficult, life-long battle, because our selfish human nature keeps interfering. To get our selfish motives out of the way, we need God's help, and He's available all the time. God's counseling center has a sign outside that says, "Walk-ins welcome. No waiting, ever. Blessings upon request."

Before we get on the mat, it's important to understand what we gain from wrestling. There are so many benefits and blessings from the spiritual practice of wrestling with God, and it's my heart's desire for you to experience these for yourself. Here are nine of them: *Freedom, healing, trust, confidence, wisdom, direction, honor, a desire to meet with God as soon as possible, and truth.*

Freedom

The first thing we gain from wrestling with God is freedom. As Jacob wrestled, he was seeking freedom from fear, his history, and his reputation. He was number one on his brother's Most Wanted List. Up to then, Jacob had done what he thought he had to do to survive – lie, cheat, steal. He was trying to steal positive self-worth, self-image, and self-approval. But to hold onto his brother's blessing, he had to run from his own.

I learned to lie, cheat and steal as a child. To survive sexual abuse, plus the incredible burden of being "perfect examples" imposed on pastor's families, I lived by the motto, "What they don't know won't hurt me." Some things I didn't have to pretend. I was an honor's student at school, and an active musician, thespian, and poet. But there was also a phony me hidden by greasepaint.

Hiding the truth cost me my freedom. I was imprisoned by the same fear I was trying to overcome. To hide my broken self, I pretended I was someone I was not. I fooled everyone except God.

The late '60's gave me some of the freedom I craved. I became a middle-class hippie – no make-up, bohemian dress, with a passionate love of Led Zeppelin and Joni Mitchell (which haven't changed). The other hippie activities went on underground. I was still an outstanding student (I love to read, write and learn to this day), still active in church (preacher's kid). On the day I graduated from college, I married my first husband and was free to live like I wanted. Appropriately attired in the business world, I did well in good jobs but still was foundering inside.

And yet, God continued to speak to my heart.

> *You will know the Truth, and the Truth will set you free. John 8:32 (AMP)*

Like Jacob, I finally discovered that truth breaks down the barricades and delivers us from the captivity of lies. Uncensored Prayer demolishes the barriers between us and God. But like Jacob, we have to be willing to struggle with God through those barriers. God's freedom was the real thing Jacob and I had always craved, and nothing would ever take it away from us again.

I passionately want this freedom for you, too, from anything that holds you captive. I don't care who you are. We all have prisons that hold us hostage at times, and God is the only one who can set us free. And God does this through Jesus. Jesus is the ultimate proof of how far God is willing to go to show us that we are loved.

> *"If the Son sets you free, you are truly free."* John 8:36 (NLT)

To discover Jesus is to realize our blessing.

Is there anything holding you back from God? Whether you believe what I'm saying or are skeptical, belligerent, or unsure, I encourage you to seek God just as you are, by yourself when it's quiet. Honestly tell Him what you think and feel, and wrestle through it. God is a jail breaker rather than a jailor, which is a whole lot better than hiding behind a lie.

Healing

The second thing we gain from wrestling with God is healing. Wounds and sickness come in many forms. I have been temporarily injured by a snub or put down, and gravely wounded by physical, mental and substance abuse. God alone chooses how and when to heal us when we humbly ask.

Sometimes Jesus healed people right on the spot.

> *And a woman who had been suffering from a hemorrhage for twelve years, came up behind Him and touched the fringe of His cloak; for she was saying to herself, "If I only touch His garment, I will get well."*
>
> *But Jesus turning and seeing her said, "Daughter, take courage; your faith has made you well." At once the woman was made well. Matthew 9:20-22 (NASB)*

What We Gain By Wrestling With God

God still performs miracles of instant healing. I know people whom God has delivered from an addiction right on the spot, and I believe He still heals physical illnesses all at once in some cases. But most healing doesn't come quickly. Most miracles are like blooming flowers, slow, and over time. They are no less miracles, just not the flashy kind.

Other healings we don't get to see. I wrestled with God for a long time in Uncensored Prayer about why miracles happened to other people, but not to me. He told me I had no idea the vast amount of miracles He had performed in my life, unknown and unseen by me. God said I would have died young if He hadn't intervened.

A major source of pain and suffering for me is my clinical depression. It's manageable with anti-depressants and good doctors, but it doesn't go away, and I've had it since junior high. Many people are afraid of mental and emotional disorders. How do you know what a "crazy" person will do? How can you trust anything they say? My favorite one is, "You should be better by now. Psychiatric therapy is just rehashing the same things again and again. Get over it!" They don't know that people with depression don't choose this disease anymore than cancer victims do. We don't want it, and can't make it just go away.

I can suddenly be sad and start crying when nothing is "wrong". I struggle with feeling insecure. At social gatherings, I often feel like I'm an outsider, clumsy with small talk. Thank God Bud and my closest friends understand, giving me love, support, and space as I need it. What keeps me on the path is God's continuous reassurance that He's with me and will help me effectively meet each challenge ahead.

In writing this book, God has asked me to risk honesty to help other people who will relate to my story of abuse, addiction, divorce or depression. If only one person finds God's hope and healing through this book, whether I ever know or not, God will honor my willingness to follow His call to this ministry. I don't believe God punished me with clinical depression. But He allowed it to happen, to bless both me and someone else.

> *God causes all things to work together for good to those who love God, to those who are called according to his purpose.*
> *Romans 8:28 (NASB)*

For Jacob, God healed one wound and gave him another. Jacob's relationship with his brother Esau was in shreds. The wound of the broken bond had never healed. Jacob must have known that if God didn't mend their relationship, he was toast. Esau was a tough outdoorsman, an area where Jacob didn't stand a chance. Jacob didn't know it, but God had already performed that miracle. Esau was ready to forgive his brother. But Jacob would never have known had he not taken the risk. He would never have discovered his own healing had he not returned home.

Now about the wound God gave Jacob.

> *This left Jacob all alone in the camp, and a man came and wrestled with him until the dawn began to break. When the man saw that he would not win the match, he touched Jacob's hip and wrenched it out of its socket. Genesis 32:24-25 (NLT)*

> *Jacob named the place Peniel (which means "face of God"), for he said, "I have seen God face to face, yet my life has been spared." The sun was rising as Jacob left Peniel, and he was limping because of the injury to his hip. Genesis32:30-31(NLT)*

Why do you suppose God gave Jacob a physical wound? He realized his need to completely depend on God. This permanent injury would always remind Jacob of the moment he discovered his blessing. Sometimes the best way for God to heal us is for us to be wounded, so that we'll reach out to Him for help.

Trust

The third thing we gain from wrestling with God is trust. Trust and faith are often thought of as synonyms, but the difference is important.

> *Behold, God, my salvation! I will **trust** and not be afraid, for the Lord God is my strength and song; yes, He has become my salvation. Isaiah 12:2 (AMP)*

> ***Faith** is the confidence that what we hope for will actually happen; it gives us assurance about things we cannot see.*

What We Gain By Wrestling With God

Through their faith, the people in days of old earned a good reputation. Hebrews 11:1-2 (NLT)

Trust is reliance on the integrity, ability and reliability of a person or thing, while faith is belief without evidence or proof. Faith is stepping out to see if God will show up. Trust is knowing God will.

Prior to Jacob's fight on the mat, his life had very little direction or meaning. His lying, cheating, and stealing had driven him from his father's land. And after twenty years of this, he just couldn't handle it anymore. So he played "Let's Make A Deal" with God.

Then Jacob made a vow, saying, "If God will be with me and will watch over me on this journey I am taking and will give me food to eat and clothes to wear so that I return safely to my father's household, then the LORD will be my God." Genesis 28:20-21 (NIV)

At this point, Jacob wasn't willing to claim the Lord as his God unless God gave in to what he wanted. Because Jacob took the initiative to seek God, he developed trust when he encountered God's blessing.

Young children usually trust someone until that person breaks their trust. As adults, we usually trust no one until they have earned our trust. I used to believe God wasn't trustworthy because I thought He always let me down because I let Him down.

As an adult, I learned to trust God by attacking Him. I was so angry at Him, and about all the crap in my life. I had yet to realize I was actually mad at myself. This is how I started practicing Uncensored Prayer. God didn't act like He was supposed to – never had. He didn't get mad at me for my attacks, and that was just…wrong. I didn't know Him at all, except that He had always been with me. A lot of good that had been, I thought.

But now God had me right where He wanted me, dumping all my pent up anger and hurt on Him. And He *blessed me for it*, just like He had done for Jacob. When I discovered God didn't blast me or punish me for my honesty, I trusted Him with more of my heart. I love this God who loves me exactly as I am. This is why I'm such an advocate for wrestling with God in Uncensored

Prayer. I've gained trust in Him that sustains me through the times I don't want to trust.

> *Trust in the Lord with all your heart;*
> *do not depend on your own understanding.*
> *Seek his will in all you do,*
> *and he will show you which path to take.* Proverbs 3:5-6 (NLT)

Confidence

The fourth thing we gain from wrestling with God is confidence. Finding out we can trust God gives us confidence to keep coming back to Him.

> *Therefore let us draw near with confidence to the throne of grace, so that we may receive mercy and find grace to help in time of need.* Hebrews 4:16 (NASB)

God doesn't just *give* us confidence, He *is* our confidence.

> *For You are my hope;*
> *O Lord GOD,* **You are my confidence.** Psalm 71:5 (NASB)

> *For* **the LORD will be your confidence**
> *And will keep your foot from being caught.* Proverbs 3:26 (NASB)

While faith is taking the risk without knowing, trust is taking the risk when we have learned through experience we can trust God. We gain confidence in God by spending time with Him through honest dialogue in Uncensored Prayer. We learn confidence by surrounding ourselves with people who know God. Thank God for people on the faith path ahead of us who are willing to help others on the same journey.

Confidence in God gives us an appropriate sense of self-confidence. For a long time my self-image was way off base. I felt I was either better than or worse than everyone else, and that would fluctuate depending on who I was with. Neither assessment was true. I wasn't a slug or a saint. I was just Joy Wilson, child of God. God informed me that His original image of me might be boring to me compared to my highly dramatic image of myself. But He knew the real, imperfect but wonderful me, and wanted me to know her, too.

Real self-confidence isn't based on comparison to other people. I am a beloved child of God who doesn't need anyone else's validation or approval for worth. I can still fall back into that old better/worse falsehood, but once I get on the mat with God, I can't stay there.

If we're wrestling with God we can't hide behind the lies. It just doesn't work. God's presence is just too penetrating. This I know for a fact: usually when I come to God, I'm squirrely about something, and leave a lot saner – a pretty good reason for honest private conversations with God.

Wisdom

The fifth thing we gain from wrestling with God is wisdom. Wisdom is seeing life from God's perspective. It's seeing what is actually true. So when we wrestle with God, stepping into His presence and light, we open ourselves up to gaining wisdom.

King Solomon is known for his wisdom. He stepped up to the plate and asked for it, and God responded by giving it to him.

Solomon didn't begin with it all together. He actually began with sacrifices to pagan gods.

> Solomon loved the LORD and followed all the decrees of his father, David, **except** that Solomon, too, offered sacrifices and burned incense at the local places of worship. The most important of these places of worship was at Gibeon, so the king went there and sacrificed 1,000 burnt offerings. 1 Kings 3:3-4 (NLT)

Then God did a highly unusual thing (He has a reputation for that). Right there at the pagan worship site.

> That night the LORD appeared to Solomon in a dream, and God said, "What do you want? Ask, and I will give it to you!" 1 Kings 3:5 (NLT)

Look at Solomon's highly unusual answer and God's response:

> *Give me an understanding heart so that I can govern your people well and know the difference between right and wrong. For who by himself is able to govern this great people of yours?"*
>
> *The Lord was pleased that Solomon had asked for wisdom. So God replied, "Because you have asked for wisdom in governing my people with justice and have not asked for a long life or wealth or the death of your enemies— I will give you what you asked for! I will give you a wise and understanding heart such as no one else has had or ever will have! And I will also give you what you did not ask for—riches and fame! No other king in all the world will be compared to you for the rest of your life! 1 Kings 3:9-13 (NLT)*

God honored Solomon's request for wisdom in a huge way. God wants to give each of us His wisdom. He knows we will make some really stupid decisions on our own without His help.

I can't begin to tell you half the bad decisions I've made because I didn't seek God's advice. Usually I thought I could handle things on my own. At times I've been reluctant to talk to God because I suspected what He'd have to say wasn't what I wanted to hear. I'm still guilty of that sometimes. The vice of rebellion is strong in this life-long hippie.

Unconsciously, the men I chose for relationships resembled my abuser – nice guys who were privately abusive. After my last divorce, I finally became aware of this pattern, and asked God to help me make healthy choices in the future.

Soon after I met Bud, he asked me out for a date. I rebuffed him. He wasn't my type, i.e. he was a nice guy who wasn't abusive. Unperturbed, Bud kept asking me out until I relented. As of this writing, we've been married 11 years, the first true marriage I've ever had. We are not only compatible, but base our relationship on God, which makes all the difference in the world.

I did not have the wisdom to choose Bud as my mate. God gave that to me, and helped me act on it. I have had to practice using that wisdom, because I was totally inexperienced in healthy relationships. I believe that God wisely knew it was time, that I was finally willing to relinquish my way of doing things, and ask for His help.

You may be aware of patterns in your life that are unhealthy, or a situation where you made a significant decision without asking for God's help, and the results were disastrous. You may be making unwise decisions right now and have no clue.

> *If any of you is deficient in wisdom, let him ask of the giving God [Who gives] to everyone liberally and ungrudgingly, without reproaching or faultfinding, and it will be given him.*
> *James 1:5 (AMP)*

I want to reassure you that God will share His wisdom with you without criticism or blaming you. I urge you to approach Him in Uncensored Prayer, because He really is a God of love, not condemning judgment, and He wants you to experience that yourself. Take your fears and questions to God, because I promise you, His wisdom is better than all of ours combined.

Direction

The sixth thing we gain from wrestling with God is direction. Direction is knowing where and when to go. When we wrestle with God, and engage Him on the mat, we can begin to ask for direction and God will surely give it to us, if we're willing to listen.

God knows He has to earn our trust for us to be willing to follow His directions. God did all kinds of things to earn the Israelites' trust, starting with parting the Red Sea after they made a hasty exit out of Egypt. They were finally ready to follow God's leadership.

> *The LORD went ahead of them. He guided them during the day with a pillar of cloud, and he provided light at night with a pillar of fire. This allowed them to travel by day or by night.*
> *Exodus 13:21 (NLT)*

> *Whether the cloud stayed above the Tabernacle for two days, a month, or a year, the people of Israel stayed in camp and did not move on. But as soon as it lifted, they broke camp and moved on. So they camped or traveled at the LORD'S command, and they did whatever the* L<small>ORD</small> *told them through Moses. Numbers 9:22-23 (NLT)*

My daddy has a lot of wisdom, much of which historically I have ignored (I told you I'm a rebel).

One time when I was out of work, daddy said, "It's God's will that we know His will. I want you to lay aside everything you think is important about your next job, including salary and previous jobs on your resume. Write down everything that is really important to you about your next job."

I got alone by myself, and asked God for direction in making this list. The first thing I wrote down was to be close to home so I could quickly get to my kids' schools if I was called to come pick up a sick child and take them home. Obviously this meant my employer would let me do this.

I also wanted a job that allowed me to come to work early in the morning and be finished by early afternoon. I've always been a morning person, which is when I'm the most alert. After about 9:00 pm I start getting sleepy and have reduced ability to function at my best. When I was young, my friends found it funny at slumber parties, which tend to last most of the night, that I fell asleep before midnight, no matter how hard I tried to stay awake. It's just how I'm wired.

Also, I longed to have a job for which I was competent. I've told you I often feel insecure, and in many of my previous jobs I had faked the capability to perform, and as a result found myself in positions where I was in way over my head, leading eventually to disaster. I could only fake it so long until it was apparent that I really didn't know what I was doing. I finally admitted to myself that I was tired of it.

Daddy reassured me that God would lead me to a position that met each of the things really important to me. That's exactly what happened, even though it paid $1/4^{th}$ of my previous position. The money was sufficient to meet my needs, and quite frankly, I needed the humbling experience of working at something I previously thought was below me. Turns out I found myself exactly where God wanted me to be so I could learn some very important life lessons.

And the time came where God made it possible for me to work at the one career which has always been my heart's desire: writing full-time. You are holding the first fruits of that dream, and it's just the beginning.

Where did God's direction lead Jacob? Into unfamiliar territory using traits he had actually had all his life, yet never used. Like me, Jacob had never been and done what he really wanted: to be someone he and other people could be proud of. To develop integrity and honesty in his relationships. To lay aside cheating and lying and gain a new identity and reputation.

Look what God has promised us when we are willing to follow His direction:

> *Delight yourself in the LORD; and He will give you the desires of your heart. Psalm 37:4 (NASB)*

Is God talking about giving us the fancy house we've always wanted? No. Is God promising to make everything perfect? Nope. Here's what is true: the more time we spend honestly with God, the more receptive we become to learning from Him and following His leadership. God's desires become our desires, which are *always* honorable and healthy. God created each of us with unique gifts, and wants to develop abilities in us we don't inherently have, so that He gets the glory for His work of transformation in us, resulting in fruit we can't produce on our own.

Honor

The seventh thing we gain from wrestling with God is honor. When we step onto the mat and engage God in Uncensored Prayer, we can begin to see that we already have God's love and respect. Honor is simply the recognition of God's love. It's acknowledging and holding onto what is already true.

The Psalms provide a unique perspective of what happens when we seek Him:

> *Because he has set his love upon Me, therefore will I deliver him; I will set him on high, because he knows and*

> understands My name [has a personal knowledge of My mercy, love, and kindness--trusts and relies on Me, knowing I will never forsake him, no, never].
>
> He shall call upon Me, and **I will answer him; I will be with him in trouble, I will deliver him and honor him.**
>
> With long life will I satisfy him and show him My salvation.
> Psalms 91:14-16(AMP)

When we call upon God, God promises to answer, to be with us, deliver us, and surprisingly, honor us. It's almost shocking to think that God wants to honor us, but that's the promise. When God honors us, He's simply reminding us of our inherent value.

Jacob took the risk to wrestle. God **answered him**, knowing he was ready to face the truth. Jacob learned he could trust God to be **with him in trouble** after wrestling all night about his fear and pain. When Jacob took the risk to meet his brother, God **delivered him** into his brother's arms. And when Jacob chose to follow God, God **honored Jacob** with blessings far beyond Jacob's imagination. God kept every one of His promises. He always does, and they are always from His heart of love.

When we choose to wrestle with God, we can begin to see that we are valuable to God. We gain respect, for both God and ourselves. Honoring what God honors is central to our growth and restoration. When we see what God sees, we can begin to live life from His perspective, which produces honor.

Honor can help us begin to stop the cycle of abuse and oppression. A common result of abuse is the victim can easily become an abuser, too. Think of the common simile of an older brother who kicks his little brother who kicks the dog. If you can't take your pain out on the person who hurt you, you might take it out on someone more defenseless than yourself. Taking such action makes you feel a bit more powerful momentarily, but the internal injury remains, undiminished and unhealed.

When a victim has been abused, it's common to lose respect for ourselves, believing in some way it was our fault. You know who I victimized? Me. If only I had fought back or told someone. I continued the cycle of violence by kicking myself with blame.

In addition to feeling my abuse was my fault, I also felt it was God's fault, too. He didn't stop it, did He? He didn't help. Why not? The boomerang invariably came back to me – it was my fault God didn't intervene. An unbroken circle in a broken heart.

By taking my brokenness to God through Uncensored Prayer, He began to restore my sense of honor for myself. I could begin to see the person God loved, and not just the broken little girl I tried to hide. By embracing God's honor, the disgrace no longer held me victim. This has been a total gift from God I hadn't been able to give myself.

> *Instead of shame and dishonor,*
> *you will enjoy **a double share of honor***
> *You will possess a double portion of prosperity in your land*
> *and everlasting joy will be yours. Isaiah 61:7 (NLT)*

God also made it very clear how He feels about me:

> *You are **precious to me**. You are honored, and **I love you**.*
> *Isaiah 43:4 (NLT)*

Are you ready to embrace the honor that God already has for you? Do you feel respect towards God? Do you attempt to treat other people the way you want to be treated? Work through this with God. Wrestle with Him, lay it all out. May you enjoy *a double share of honor*, because **He loves you, precious one.**

A Desire To Meet With God Again

The eighth thing we gain from wrestling with God is a desire to meet with Him again. Once we step onto the mat and engage God in Uncensored Prayer, we can begin to see restoration and growth. Relationship with God becomes something we crave, as opposed to something we ignore. We learn that God is someone with whom we can share our most intimate secrets, and God won't hold it against us.

A few years ago, and after seven years of sobriety, I started drinking again.

The person I most dreaded telling was Bud. We had met shortly before I had gotten sober, and married a year later. Having both been previously married, Bud and I made commitments to place God first in our relationship and to make our marriage a number one priority, never taking for granted our need to remain honest and close.

Unlike my marriage, I began taking my sobriety for granted as time went by, gradually becoming lax in practicing my program of recovery. Ignoring all the wise words of warning from people with long-term sobriety, I became cocky, certain I had this thing licked.

Just like I had been told, the day came where I had no defense against my addiction, and drank again. I think deep down I had expected this to happen one day, but still was taken by surprise with the suddenness of my actions.

My marriage was succeeding because of God's help and our mutual daily focus on treating each other with love and respect. What frightened me was I didn't know how Bud would react. Would my action erect a permanent barrier between us? I valued our closeness, and was afraid this would jeopardize everything we had built together. The only way I could find out for sure was to tell Bud.

I knew another alcoholic could tell someone was drinking in a heartbeat, yet I had this insane idea I could hide it from him. We had agreed not to lie to each other – a destructive part of our previous marriages – and I knew I had the power to tear down something precious between Bud and me. Would I take the risk of being honest with Bud? I finally decided I had to, no matter what the consequences might be. I just couldn't bear the thought of another marriage destroyed by deceit.

Bud's response to the news was obviously disappointment and sadness, but not blame. He assured me of his love, no matter what. He said, "I ain't going nowhere." Relief and gratitude overwhelmed me, and when I became willing, I got sober again. Then the day came when I drank again. Now how would Bud react? Would he forgive me again? With trepidation I admitted my fall. Bud's response was the same.

Over the years, I have gone through periods of drinking and not drinking, back and forth. I want to and don't want to. You'll read about my struggle in the second section of this book. I don't trust myself in this area. People with long-term sobriety, like Bud, say there's no guarantee they won't be blindsided by this disease someday and actively use again. No addict is exempt from this possibility. I mentally concede to this truth, and yet...

I still don't comprehend it when Bud says, "I ain't going nowhere" when I fall again. I keep waiting for the last straw to break. I'm astounded by his commitment to me, not only to stay with me, but to refuse a marriage of convenience. He knows my determination to fight fiercely for the kind of marriage I've never had before. I believe I would forgive anything Bud might do down the road. Obviously, no one knows for sure how they'll react in the future. But the willingness we both have to fight for something precious at all cost is the strength of our bond.

The way Bud consistently forgives me when I fail – even the times I've confessed I've lied to him – makes me want to be with him even more, and has given me the courage to tell him the truth when I fail. In spite of my disappointment in myself and the sadness I know this causes Bud, I know from experience it's safe to be honest with him.

Do you know who he's acting like? God. Of course Bud is imperfect, unlike our perfect Daddy. There have been many, many times Bud has failed me and himself, and I've chosen to forgive him. God's unfailing response of love and forgiveness to my confessions of sin and failure when I've come to Him in Uncensored Prayer has made me eager to come to Him every time. God has earned my trust, and I am convinced He will never judge or abandon me, no matter what.

The desire Bud and I have as best friends to talk over secrets, questions and pain is magnified a hundred fold by our interactions with God through wrestling in Uncensored Prayer. God is the ultimate listener. I can tell Him anything and He won't hold it against me. I crave that and value it deeply. As I've learned I can trust God, my desire for seeking out God has grown ten-fold. I *want* to wrestle with God. I *want* to share what is on my heart, because I know God won't shame me. God is right there to love me, even when I've blown it. God never loses site of my value, even when I do.

I know I'm just a person who has told you God is safe to trust with whatever we feel and say. Like me, you might believe at this point, "Sure, that's been your experience with God, in spite of your troubled background, but I don't know He'll respond that way to me." I understand how you feel. That belief about God kept me from trusting Him for a long, long time.

I don't ask or expect you to accept or believe anything I say in this book. I'm no authority here. But my conviction comes from personal experience. I've stepped onto the mat with God and shared my heart in Uncensored Prayer, and God stayed with me. And the only way for you to experience this is to try it for yourself. God values your trust, too, and wants talk privately with you again as soon as possible.

You can't take my word for it. The only way you can find out for yourself is to take the risk of an unedited conversation with God. This isn't any of my business, but please try it.

Truth

The ninth thing we gain from wrestling with God is a sense of truth. As we go through life, it's so easy to get stuck in the destructive grasp of the lie that says, "You are just not worth it." It captivates us and eats at our soul. It destroys us from the inside because we learn to think it's true. Destroying that lie is one of the most important things we accomplish on the mat. And when we do, we can learn to live a life based on what is true, what is honest.

I recently had the opportunity to share a few of my Uncensored Prayers before a group that included several preachers. Afterwards, one pastor came up to me and said, "You have just slapped me up the side of my head with the realization of how selective my prayers are with God. You're right – I don't tell God what I think, because I believe some of my thoughts are blasphemous, disrespectful and unacceptable to a holy God. I thought I was an expert on prayer, and now I think I have a lot to learn." So do we all.

Look what God promises us when we seek Him in Uncensored Prayer:

> *I will reveal to them an abundance of peace and truth.*
> *Jeremiah 33:6 (NASB)*

What are we actually receiving when God gives us peace and truth? God Himself.

What We Gain By Wrestling With God

> *Jesus said to him, I am the Way and the Truth and the Life; no one comes to the Father except by (through) Me. John 14:6 (AMP)*

As we spend time completely honest with God, He reveals truth to us, because Jesus is Truth. Facing reality may be difficult and painful, but God's promise makes it worth it.

> *Come to Me, all you who labor and are heavy-laden and overburdened, and I will cause you to rest. [I will ease and relieve and refresh your souls.]*
>
> *Take My yoke upon you and learn of Me, for I am gentle (meek) and humble (lowly) in heart, and you will find rest (relief and ease and refreshment and recreation and blessed quiet) for your souls.*
>
> *For My yoke is wholesome (useful, good--not harsh, hard, sharp, or pressing, but comfortable, gracious, and pleasant), and My burden is light and easy to be borne. Matthew 11:28-30 (AMP)*

By taking the risk of wrestling with God, we will gain freedom and healing that comes from seeing reality. God has never stopped loving us. God has always been there in the midst of our pain and suffering. We just couldn't see it.

> *You will know the Truth, and the Truth will set you free. John 8:32 (AMP)*

The awesome gifts that God has given me as I've practiced wrestling with Him astound me. I had no idea what was waiting for me when I started this spiritual practice. No one taught me how to pray like this. I found out on my own. I'm sharing my experiences with you in this book because of the way it's transformed my life, and perhaps this spiritual practice has never occurred to you. My prayer is you will have your own unedited experience with God, because I believe it will change your life for the good.

Truth begins with getting honest with ourselves. This is where Uncensored

Prayer starts. But learning to step onto the mat requires developing a sense of honesty in a practical way. It starts with admitting that our pain and suffering are destroying us. But it also begins with admitting that we are worth fighting for, that there is honor and dignity in the self.

I don't believe there's anyone out there who doesn't wish they had more freedom, healing, trust, confidence, wisdom, direction, honor, and truth. Some people wish they could really trust someone with the truth about themselves without judgment. Some people long for direction in their lives because they feel they're floating around aimlessly. Their life lacks meaning and purpose, and they wish God was someone they could trust, but they aren't sure about that, and are afraid to find out, in case God will blow them away, and they don't know if they could handle rejection again.

What do you want to do about it? What are you willing to do about it?

Chapter 4

The Cost Of Wrestling With God

As we develop an understanding of what we can gain by wrestling with God, it is also critical to recognize what we lose. Wrestling with God in Uncensored Prayer has a cost. As we step into an uncensored life, we begin to recognize that some things get left behind. But ultimately the costs are the things that oppress us and cause us pain and suffering. The cost of wrestling with God is then as important as what we gain.

The cost of wrestling with God may sound like a negative. It's cost me a lot to risk vulnerability and honesty with God. Risk itself is costly because of the unknown, which may turn out to be *really* bad. Lord knows I've taken tons of risks in life resulting in painful disasters. But the only way you're going to find out if the cost of wrestling with God is worth the risk is to try it for yourself.

The cost of wrestling with God is actually a positive. When we step onto the mat, we can begin to let go of our fears, our wants, and our crippling desires that never worked anyway. On the mat we learn to let go of: *Pride, our comfort zone, dependency on traditions, fear of God, and fear of what people will think.*

Pride

The first thing we have to lose is our pride. Pride is our failed attempt at finding honor in something other than God. It's rooted in the desire to be like God, which we can never do. To give up pride is to rediscover the honor that God has always provided.

When we step onto the mat, God wants us to bring all of our struggles, so we can wrestle with Him. God likes a good fight. Pride keeps many of us from being honest with God, which is silly, because He already knows what we think. For our own sake, God wants us to name what we want and why we want to talk with Him. That takes laying aside pride – pretending we have our act together – and humbling ourselves to admit the truth of sin or shame. It's only when we get really honest that we're able to hear God be honest with us.

In order for Jacob to return home, he had to let go of his pride. Stealing the blessing never really worked anyway. Jacob spent close to twenty years in isolation, away from the land of his fathers. And the only way to return home was to admit the truth. He had to face the reality that what he had done didn't work. But in letting go of pride, he gained his identity. He gained a sense of hope about what God was doing in his life. He got to reconcile with his brother.

Letting go of pride isn't easy. I've failed more times that I like to admit, but when I admit it, I'm free of pride's captivity. It's a terrible taskmaster because it's unrelenting. It demands perfection and refuses grace at every turn. But it is possible to let it go.

The best-paying job I've ever had came with enormous responsibility. I excel at detail work, and as the tradeshow manager of an international company, it was my responsibility to negotiate contracts with hotels and convention centers, sell booth space, assign meeting rooms, hire entertainment, work with event staff planning menus, order AV equipment, etc.

However, I was ill-suited to handle the big stuff. My people management skills are negligible, and during tradeshow weeks hundreds of people would report to me. The responsibility overwhelmed me. To make things worse, I had trouble handling all the free booze at parties, business luncheons, and placed in my suite. It seems it was obvious to everyone but me that I was often drunk on the job.

I covered my inadequacies with prideful bossiness, and was known as the "Bitch From Hell". I thought acting arrogant gave me the professional edge to get people to do what I wanted. Instead, it had the opposite effect.

My business deficits outweighed my strengths, and after two years I was given the choice of resigning or being fired the week before Christmas. Ho ho ho. Looking back, failing at that job was one of the best things that ever happened to me.

To stay afloat, I sought work through a temporary agency, and was placed as a secretary covering a pregnancy leave-of-absence. When that ended, the agency placed me as the receptionist in a very small CPA firm. Talk about the fall of the "mighty".

> *Pride ends in humiliation, while humility brings honor.*
> *Proverbs 29:23 (NLT)*

Failing miserably forced me back to the mat. I cried out to God all my shame and pain in Uncensored Prayer. I hadn't done that as a highly paid manager – "I can handle this on my own, God, thank you very much." As a good psychotherapist, God listened compassionately without judgment. Then gently, He began confronting me about how pride had been my downfall. Pride had cost me my job, which humiliated me. I felt additional humiliation having to take low-paying clerical positions just to buy groceries. I came to Him humbly and found redemption and grace. God was willing to listen as much as talk. He didn't shame me but instead wrapped me in His arms and reminded me I was worth it.

Our Comfort Zone

The second thing we lose is our comfort zone. When we wrestle with God and engage in Uncensored Prayer, we lose our capacity to stay safe and comfortable in what oppresses us, in what causes us pain and suffering. We lose the capacity to sit idly by, bored stiff, and wondering if there is any meaning to life.

Losing our comfort zone can be both scary and exhilarating, because we never know in advance what the result will be, and we may not like it. It makes it easier for us to follow Him, even when it's one step forward, two steps back, when we know God will dance that same direction with us, even though it often seems bizarre.

God is much crazier than me, which makes it easier to follow Him, because I *know* I'm crazy. I know I need help that I haven't been able to find anywhere else but with God. Jesus came to earth not just to save us from our own self-destruction, but to let us know what Daddy God is like. I believe God reveals the aspects of His character to each individual according to what they need to believe in Him.

Look at the different ways Jesus healed people. He used the method that person needed to believe. Some people needed Jesus to touch them. A sick woman just needed to touch Jesus' robe. A paralytic may not have believed at all, but his friends did, and Jesus healed the guy because of his friends. Jesus put mud on a blind man's eyes and told him to wash it off, which is kind of weird, but it was what it took for that man to believe. Some people needed odd things; other people simply needed Jesus to say the word. We're all different, and God meets us where we are for our healing. But for us to grow, we have to follow God out of our comfort zone. Every time.

Jacob had to step out of his comfort zone to have a transforming experience with God. Exile was comfortable until he recognized he was missing out on his family. He didn't appear to have very much personal experience with God. His dad and granddad were the prayer experts in the family. Jacob's comfort zone was manipulating people and doing what he damn well pleased. He even tried to manipulate God.

Writing this book was a huge leap out of my comfort zone and into the Grand Canyon while God stood on the cliff waving goodbye (at least I thought). God told me He was my agent for my book, and my part was to do what He and my editor told me to do, and God would take care of the results. Writing required me to step into areas where I had zero experience and knowledge. Yes, I was afraid, but I stepped out of my comfort zone because God said He would take care of everything, including giving me the courage to take what felt like an insane act of faith.

Stepping out of our comfort zone means we get to embrace our freedom. It allows us to experience the thrill of the life God has always wanted us to know. Makes you want to sign up for your own custom-made experience off the cliff, doesn't it. I promise you it isn't easy. Following God never is. I also promise you it's worth the risk.

Dependency On Traditions

The third thing we lose is our dependency on traditions. Traditions are wonderful, even sacred things that bind us together with the past and each other. Rituals can offer great solace in a transient world and society that alters over time. But the same traditions that give us meaning are the very same traditions that bind us. We learn not to step out of bounds because tradition says so. We're resistant to revise or abandon traditions, because they're familiar. With all the variables in life, continuity can feel like a safe haven. Even changing what's destructive or outgrown is difficult, because change brings the unknown.

To step outside of tradition is revolutionary and will attract opposition and scorn from many people. Starting a new tradition is much easier than trying to modify an established one. It can be dangerous – look at Martin Luther and Martin Luther King. Martin Luther chose to step outside the traditions of the Catholic Church and was excommunicated for it. Martin Luther King chose to step outside the traditions of segregated culture and was murdered for it.

Although Jesus practiced and honored the Jewish traditions, he also changed our perspective of them.

> *"Don't misunderstand why I have come. I did not come to abolish the law of Moses or the writings of the prophets. No, I came to accomplish their purpose."* Matthew 5:17 (NLT)

His life and message radically altered everything.

> *Therefore if anyone is in Christ, he is a new creature; the old things passed away; behold, new things have come.* 2 Corinthians 5:17 (NASB)

One of the unusual things God likes to do is speak to us through unexpected sources. Moses heard God through a burning bush in Exodus 3. Paul actually saw Jesus on the road to Damascus (Acts 9). But my favorite Biblical non-traditional message from God was to a guy named Balaam, found in Numbers 22.

Balaam was taking a trip against God's instructions, so the Lord sent an angel to block his path. Balaam's donkey saw the angel, and refused to budge. Balaam's response was to beat his animal several times. Finally the donkey had had enough.

> *And the LORD opened the mouth of the donkey, and she said to Balaam, "What have I done to you, that you have struck me these three times?"* Numbers 22:28 (NASB)

Then Balaam argued with the donkey until God opened his eyes to see the angel. I think it's hilarious that God spoke through a donkey, and even stranger that Balaam had a conversation with the animal.

God can talk to us through anything: a movie, song, book, or the microwave if He wants to. But I promise you that God will make sure we know it's from Him. He isn't going to let us think we're crazy.

In the non-traditional ways God may speak to us, He never eradicates any forms of worship that accurately reveal Him. As we get to know God better through the spiritual practice of wrestling with God, He opens up all kinds of new ways to experience Him. In my Uncensored Prayer times with God, He continues to alter my image of Him, and as unsettling as that is at times, I know I can count on God to do the unexpected. I'm interested in seeing what He'll do next. God is the ultimate revolutionary.

It's interesting that God allowed Jacob to continue practicing his family's religious rituals. There is no indication that he ever left that path. God didn't want Jacob's concept of appropriate worship traditions to interfere with Jacob having a personal relationship with Him. What God did was expand what Jacob knew about Him, and continued to enhance Jacob's understanding of his true self and God's desire to enrich his life. I believe Jacob persistently sought God through Uncensored Prayer because of how God blessed him.

My own family's worship rituals were set in concrete, since my daddy was an evangelical conservative pastor. I crawled out from under my rock rebellious and set out to create my own way of doing things. As an adult, I joined a variety of churches from different denominations and non-denominations, and went through periods of my life where I didn't attend church at all. Who needs church, you know?

The Cost Of Wrestling With God

And then about ten years ago, a very scary thing happened to my comfort zone of religious traditions. Over a relative brief period of time, all the bells and whistles in church lost meaning for me, and this was when I was an active member of a church. Communion and all the other sacraments of the church just dropped off my radar screen, no longer giving me comfort. I doubted everything I had previously believed and was left with nothing – a total, bottomless religious void. Scared the crap out of me.

I went to God and we wrestled big time about it. Here I had come back to church after a long time of wandering around, and now...

"What's up with this, God?" I asked. "What are you doing to me?" God's response was my traditions had become more important to me than my relationship with Him. God temporarily cancelled what I thought was meaningful about church so He could get my attention, and help me refocus on Him alone.

Our worship traditions may be very significant and powerful for each of us, or even non-existent. I honor your beliefs. But I challenge dependency on any tradition that hinders us from a fresh encounter with God. We can safely talk about all of this with God. My experience with God is He doesn't condemn or judge anything we discuss or question. Don't hold back with Him. He isn't going to hold back with you.

Let me know if God messes with your traditions by bringing you a talking donkey. I'd like to meet her.

Fear Of God

The fourth thing we lose is our fear of God. And I know what you are thinking. "But we're supposed to fear God." Our minds instantly race to the verse in Proverbs that says,

> The *fear of the LORD* is the beginning of knowledge.
> Proverbs 1:7

A healthy sense of fear is always a good place to start, but not if it keeps us from engaging in an honest, life-giving relationship with God. If our only view is one of a terrifying God out there, we'll never comprehend the kind of relationship that Jesus suggested we could have.

To lose the fear is to gain a deep sense of respect and wonder of a God who is deeply interested in our restoration.

> *For you have not received a spirit of slavery leading to fear again, but you have received a spirit of adoption as sons by which we cry out, "Abba! Father!" Romans 8:15 (NASB)*

Abba means "daddy" in Aramaic, like a child would say. *Abba* is what Jesus called his Daddy in Uncensored Prayer. When you spend personal time with God, you'll lose your fear of Him, and realize He's your Daddy, too.

There's something else that's very important to understand when you read "fear of God" in the Bible. Some words and phrases are impossible to translate accurately from one language to another.

> *You shall follow the LORD your God and **fear Him**; and you shall keep His commandments, listen to His voice, serve Him, and cling to Him. Deuteronomy 13:4 (NASB).* Another translation says, *"him you must **revere**" (NIV).*

> *Honor all people, love the brotherhood, **fear God**, honor the king. 1 Peter 2:17 (NASB)*

The same verse in a different translation:

> *Show respect for all men [treat them honorably]. Love the brotherhood (the Christian fraternity of which Christ is the Head). **Reverence God**. Honor the emperor. (AMP)*

When it says "**fear God**" in the Bible, it means "**reverent respect**". Makes a big difference, doesn't it. Time alone with God will eliminate your fear of Him, and replace it with reverence and respect. It took me awhile to have my ingrained fear of God removed, but that was something God proved to me. We can love and respect a God who loves us instead of judges us, and that's what He's like.

I feared God big-time when I first assaulted Him in Uncensored Prayer. My pain overcame my dread of His retaliation. That's what I expected of God. I fully expected God to be ashamed of me for how much I sinned, or didn't get it right. I could come to the altar at church and confess my sin. But God help me if I did it again. That meant I either wasn't sincere the first time, or didn't believe. My constant pattern of sin, confess, sin, confess went on and on, until the confessions stopped because of this verse:

If I regard iniquity in my heart, the Lord will not hear me.
Psalm 66:18 (AMP)

I couldn't or wouldn't give up my use of addictive substances, promiscuity and abusive behavior, so I was screwed with God. Why even try talking to Him, since He wasn't going to hear me anyway. I never would have gone to God with my anger and pain until I reached the end of my rope. He was going to blast me anyway, but I wanted to tell Him how I felt, whether He listened to me or not.

Fear is debilitating, no matter the source. And fear of God is a barrier between us that only we can choose to cross. The only way to get past that is to approach Him through unedited prayer. All the promises in the world aren't going to convince you until you take the risk yourself.

Well? Will you?

Fear Of What Other People Will Think.

The fifth thing we lose is our fear of what other people will think. This last one is a doozey. I'm a Lone Ranger, who at first doesn't care what other people think about me, and then I do, and then I don't. It's a vicious cycle. I've been a people pleaser for much of my life. I've felt that if I just did or said the right thing, I could earn acceptance. It often didn't work, but I kept trying anyway, because I wanted so badly to be accepted and believed.

One of my risks in writing this book is some of you are going to disagree with me to the extreme, and that is your right. To reach the people who will benefit by my message, I have to accept the challenge of those threatened and upset by what I say. My primary solace, strength and affirmation will come from God. Other Jesus-followers already love and support me, no matter what. That is a great encouragement.

Part of the reason Jacob wrestled was because he was afraid of what his brother Esau might do to him in their upcoming encounter. I would certainly be scared by someone who promised to kill me the last time we met. Fear of

Esau drove Jacob to wrestle with God about it. That was the best thing Jacob could have done, because that was where he found comfort, encouragement, and reassurance to face his brother, even though Jacob *still* didn't know if Esau intended to kill him. Knowing that God was with him made all the difference in the world.

Scripture is filled with people overcoming what other people think. When the angel Gabriel appeared to the Virgin Mary, announcing that she was pregnant with God's Son, she didn't know what to think about this startling message. Gabriel told Mary who Jesus was: the Son of God given authority as King of Kings forever. He told her not to be afraid.

> *For nothing is impossible with God. Luke 1:37 (NLT)*

As an example, Gabriel announced God had caused Mary's relative, Elizabeth, to become pregnant, even though she was old. Mary's response was one of joy.

> *"I am the Lord's servant," Mary answered. "May your word to me be fulfilled." Luke 1:38 (NIV)*

Then she immediately ran to see Elizabeth, excited to tell her the good news.

I wish Scripture told us more about Mary's three month visit with her relative. When did reality set in? For Mary, the pregnancy meant tremendous public scorn, possibly death by stoning. What would her parents say? Would Joseph reject her? At some point, Mary had to think, "What is God doing to me? Was I insane to agree to this?" I bet she and God had a world-class wrestling match on the mat with Uncensored Prayer. We like to think of Mary as pious and demure, but I think she was more than that.

What if God selected her for this challenge of faith and commitment because she was a fighter? I think the key to her courage was she knew that even though Gabriel had left, God hadn't and wouldn't. He was her partner, and she knew she could trust Him to help her handle everything that lay ahead. Mary was one of the three women who had the courage at stand at the foot of the cross watching Jesus die, even though every one of the disciples except John had abandoned him. She had faith in God that overcame her fear.

And so can you!

The Cost Of Wrestling With God

Do you want to make God ecstatic? Risk Uncensored Prayer. I'm usually not ecstatic about it. I still have fear issues with God, and question Him a lot. But I'm learned that's OK – something I've ached for a long, lonely time. I've discovered I please Him when I take the risk to trust Him. And then I discover God is already pleased with me; He loves me and accepts me as I am, which enables me to learn from Him and grow.

What are you willing to give up to gain the blessings found in the spiritual practice of wrestling with God? Are you open to stepping beyond your comfort zone and dependency on traditions? God will never force you to do what He suggests. He will accept you where you are, whether you're willing to follow Him in spiritual growth or not.

I have come to believe that if we *never* move past where we are, God's OK with that. He knows what we're like. He knows what we're going to do. Now, why would God create some people He knew would never accept His call, never believe in Him or follow Him? I have no clue. He just chooses to do things this way.

I can't comprehend why He accepts and loves us no matter what. All I can figure out is God values us having free-will to choose Him or not. No one, not even God, can make us love a person, tennis, or spinach. Either we do or we don't.

When we choose to wrestle with God, when we engage in Uncensored Prayer, it will cost us what we initially think matters most. It will cost us our pride, comfort zone, dependency on traditions, our fear of God, and our fear of what people will think. But isn't that what we're trying to get rid of any way?

God is willing to reach out to us regardless of what it costs Him. My experience with Uncensored Prayer is what I've gained has far outweighed the cost to me. I encourage you to risk whatever you're able and go to God, just as you are, whether you believe it will be worth it or not. Just go and find out for yourself.

SECTION 2

GETTING ON THE MAT

Uncensored Prayer is a totally honest conversation with God, in our own language, coming to God just as we are. God doesn't want a one-way message from us, and He won't speak to us if we aren't willing to listen. He wants dialogue *with* us, and that has become one of the most meaningful things in my life.

In this second section, I will share with you examples of how I wrestle with God in Uncensored Prayer. Each of us has a personal invitation from the ultimate Counselor to get on the mat and wrestle through our fear, pain, anger, and doubt. No appointment needed. No waiting in line. But it isn't free.

Getting on the mat with God requires our willingness to be completely honest while we talk with God. And He will treat us the same way, because when we listen with an open heart, we can hear God's heart, too. He can teach us if we are teachable. He will reach us if we are willing to be reached.

To begin the spiritual practice of wrestling with God, pray what you've always wanted to ask God, but were afraid to ask. Tell God how you feel. Be yourself. No one else is listening but God, and He will never reject, criticize, or leave you.

Whatever we say truthfully to God is holy, because God is Truth, and He values truth from us. There is no right or wrong way to pray. Isn't that wonderful news? Isn't that scary as hell? I know what you mean. Been there, am there.

I usually talk with God when we are alone together and can hear each other.

Another meaningful way I pray is by writing down my thoughts, as I've done here. Sometimes I just want to tell God what I feel and think. Other times God engages in dialogue with me while I write.

My writings are a window into my soul, a diary of my honest conversations with God, never really meant for anyone to read but me. My language is very personal, ranging from beautiful to raw. All I've done is be honest with God.

So why have I shared these deeply personal conversations with you? To illustrate how I wrestle with God through Uncensored Prayer. Sometimes we need examples to give us a start. I've shared them to give you a start into the process.

How you would engage in this spiritual practice might be very different from mine. If you need to begin with mine, that's fine, but I want to encourage you to discover your own words, your own voice. You might be very tentative at first, trusting God with only a morsel of truth. He will be delighted. My experience has been the more I get on the mat bringing only truth with me, the more truth I bring with me next time.

God wants to wrestle *with* us, not beat us up. He fights fair, even when we don't. God won't make us tell Him anything or do whatever He suggests. He honors our free-will, because He made us that way.

Allow God to speak to your heart in this section, and talk with Him about it like you've always wanted to do. I suggest not focusing on whether you agree with what I say or how I say it. Just listen to God. He has something to say to you.

Chapter 5

Letting Go Of Dishonesty

Practicing Uncensored Prayer means being completely honest with God and yourself. Honesty is necessary to understand truth, and truth often hurts. That's a motivation for some people to avoid Uncensored Prayer. It's painful to face reality about ourselves and our lives, past and present. I've found it's even painful to face the positive things, because feeling like a screw-up is normal for many of us. Healing requires change, and that can be terrifying. Here's a verse that gives a good reason to struggle with God:

> *Do not be anxious about anything, but in every situation, by prayer and petition, with thanksgiving, present your requests to God. And the peace of God, which transcends all understanding, will guard your hearts and your minds in Christ Jesus. Philippians 4:6-7 (NIV)*

Disaster was my pathway to peace, and sometimes talking with God today still feels like impending disaster. I'm shocked at times with what I say to Him. It feels risky. I'm still waiting to break the last straw, for God's patience with me to expire. My old image of a wrathful, unapproachable God isn't dead, just buried in an inner dungeon. Satan, the ultimate lie-spinner, drags that scary "God" back up in me when he knows I'm vulnerable to doubt, and very effectively bludgeons my faith.

But the minute I start tip-toeing up to God in censored prayer, He jumps in my face and says, "We aren't going to play that game, girl. Come on, talk straight with me. What's going on?"

Letting Go Of Dishonesty

I want to warn you that if you start practicing Uncensored Prayer, it will ruin your ability to be less than honest with God anymore. God won't let you. He's waited all your life for you to lay down pretense with Him. When it comes to God, the cliché "You can run, but you can't hide" is true.

Because God became personal to me when I was very young, I've always been aware that He's been with me, quietly biding His time until I was willing to face Him dead on. The day my anger and pain exploded all over God, I attacked Him. I felt I had nothing left to lose. I was already condemned, and I didn't care anymore.

I was totally unprepared for God to fight back. Expecting obliteration, I found confrontation instead. Little did I know that God wasn't fighting me – He was fighting *for* me. I was fighting *myself*, but didn't know it. Even as I write this, my eyes are blurred with tears, remembering that desperation and pain. I wanted to matter to God, but also to matter to myself. I wanted it bad enough to risk everything, risk going to hell that day instead of later.

I didn't know God finally had me where He'd wanted me all along – I had surrendered to God for the first time in my life. There was nothing humble about it. I didn't know how to be humble to God, only afraid.

I didn't realize it at the time, but I had just discovered and experienced that surrendering to God requires wrestling with Him, involving Uncensored Prayer without heeding the possible consequences. Desperation overruled timidity, because I finally wanted to find out if God really loved me or not. I had been thoroughly indoctrinated that God loved me in spite of my sin, which was something I *did*. What I really wanted to know was did God love me for *who I was, as I was* – even if I never changed, even if I never pleased Him like the "saints" who humbly followed the rules.

The shock of my life was I learned God was already pleased with me. When He made me, He knew I was flawed, and He didn't toss me in the trash and start over. God chose not to make robots, but unpredictable varmints who had the ability to chose or reject Him. *God wanted desperately for me to love Him for who He was, as He was, more than for anything He did.* The Lord of the Universe wanted unconditional love from *me* as much as I wanted it from Him.

Can you take that in? Did you know that's true about you and God, too?

Do you want this badly enough to find out for yourself?

In this section, I reveal how Uncensored Prayer delivers me from the bondage of lies. Our misconceptions about God can distance us from Him. Lies that we believe about ourselves keep us from knowing our true worth as children of God. By letting go of dishonesty, we can experience that truth is liberating and wonderful.

Incomprehensible Love

I've been reading up on you
and you're the most inconsistent person I know.

You claim to be a God of perfect goodness,
yet you get away with bloody murder –
destroying individuals and entire people groups
while calling yourself the epitome of peace and love.

Everything you think you know about me is wrong.

So you're not all about love, after all.
I've been a complete fool to trust you.

No, you're a complete human.
You have no true concept
of what love and goodness are.

I've told you it's impossible
for you to understand my ways.
I'm completely consistent and fair,
which you're incapable of understanding.

You are really pissing me off right now.
I thought you were my best friend
and now you're calling me a dumbshit.

Whoa, wait a minute...

No, YOU wait a minute.
It's taken me a long time
to learn to trust you,
to believe you really love me
and now I find out it's all a lie.

Will you listen to me for a bit?

No.

Fine. I'll talk to the doorknob.
Doorknob, what I think and do
will make absolutely no sense to you.

I don't fit into any category.
You slap a nametag on me that says,
"Hello, my name is LOVE,"
and because the dictionary says love means
"a deep devotion and affection for someone,"
you've decided that means I'm kind and faithful
according to your expectations.

Well, love doesn't mean acting hateful and lying.

I thought you weren't listening.

Well, the doorknob and I agree
you can't be loving and hateful at the same time.

You're confusing actions with identity.
Acting out of love sometimes means causing pain.

I understand that.

Look how you're feeling right now.

Betrayed and used.

How so?

You said you're not who I thought you were.

That's true.
But that doesn't mean I've lied to you.
You're taking my grand plan for the universe personally.
The close relationship between you and me
is exactly what you believed yesterday.
We share deep love and respect for each other,
and I've proven trustworthy.
I have not, and will not renege on that.
Everything you believe about me
as your best friend is bulls-eye accurate.

But to use this as THE definition of love
is far from true.
Humans aren't capable of comprehending
all the aspects and dynamics of love.

Letting Go Of Dishonesty

*Many of my actions and choices
seem to be the opposite of love.*

Well, cruelty and kindness aren't the same thing.

I agree.

But sometimes what may seem cruel to you
is actually a link in the love chain,
created for the benefit of the whole world.

That sounds so wrong,
and it makes you look like a terrible God.

*It can't be helped.
It's the truth that all I do – ALL – is love.*

You give me a headache.

*I have a cure for that.
Trust what you have learned from me
with the faith I've given you,
and stop trying to figure out the rest.
Celebrate what we share together,
and leave the universe to me.*

You can have it.

Thanks…I already do.

The Lunge of Faith, Part 1

Catch me if you can.

What's this "can" crap?

OK, catch me if you will.

Who's the unwilling one here?
Do you want to live free or not?

Yes.

You know the price.

I must jump into the invisible,
trusting I'll fall into your arms.

What if it's like falling in love?
You'll never know unless it happens to you.

You make it sound so easy.

It isn't. Love is very expensive.
Love is gentle and kind – you know these things.
What you fear is giving up control
to gain the best in you and receive the best from me.
Staying miserable by hanging onto what you know for sure
is a horrible way to live.
Am I right?

No one knows this better than me.

It's like a tattoo shop with a sign outside
that says, "Yes, it hurts,"
but people are willing to pay with pain
to gain their choice of beauty.
What would you pay to feel beautiful deep inside
without shame or blame for yourself?
Child, I don't think you realize
you fear yourself more than me.
You truly don't love yourself
or know your self-value.

I only know what I see.

*Those who love you see who you really are:
a person of great worth with faults,
perhaps different from theirs.
Now about tomorrow –
why not take a lunge of faith?*

What if it doesn't work?

*What if it does?
Will you risk 24 hours to prove my point?*

I'll try…

You've proven a million times that doesn't work.

I SAID I'll try –
I know I can do that.

*I promise I'll help you
if you'll just do it.*

Well…OK.

Deal.

The Lunge of Faith, Part 2

So how did it work out?

Why do you always want me to tell you
what you already know?

To see if you really know it for yourself.
You believe what you name out-loud
and with practice, it becomes a bedrock belief.
Did I help you yesterday?
You did your part with your lunge of faith
and didn't jump backwards into the known.
Are you willing to stay here with me tomorrow?

You mean I have to do this again?

It's not "Again."
You're already here safe with me.

Well, I certainly don't feel safe.

All I ask is one more day.

And then?

You'll see.

Seeing in the Dark

Out under the stars,
all four of them,
as black velvet fades in the dawn,
I still wish on the million stars unseen
but known, all named by you.

And I breathe in faith
I will need later when I can't see you
and think you can't see me.
My rocky journey in the dark
is often only lit by memory
and faith that you are still out there,
still here, still inside me.

Sometimes it feels when I cry for you
that only the trees can hear,
which is true enough,
for you indwell all of your creation.
Help my faith to spread like cancer
eating me alive, until all that's left of unbelief
are four stars fading to light.

Listening Love

Extraordinary error envelopes me,
mails me to the South Pole
to the end of my toes.
In reflux rebound, my stomach revolts,
complains to my brain, "I hate how this feels"
with no repeal to the God I love
who appears to be out to lunch –
thanks a bunch.

I know this is mite size
compared to the martyrs –
the saints who succeeded
at humility love joy peace patience kindness etc. –
inconsistent attributes I long to live for real,
reflecting the grace of God so undeserved by me.

Are you back yet, God?

I know you never leave,
but sometimes I can't sense you listening patiently to me,
though some believe it isn't right
to talk like this to a righteous God.

But you already know what I think
and want me to tell the truth to you,
no matter what it is.

Thanks for letting me be honest
when I whine and gripe "This isn't fair,"
when I'm a jerk and childish
and feel nobody cares.

Thanks for listening and loving me
when I feel like I've blown it
and I don't respect myself.

You patiently restore me until I can start anew
to persevere through failure
and forgive myself as faulty,
but redeemed and strong and true.

One Step Off the Path

Where did you go, God?
Back space...
where did I go?
Sideways, backways,
wrapped in the familiar,
following tried and failed paths
that lead to lonely, lost and lies.
I see you, just ahead, leading,
feel your spirit here, loving,
know you've got my back,
indwell my fear.

You trust your hope for me,
even though I hesitate
to trust you with my happiness.
I know I'm sick,
but I'm comfortable with guilt.
I'm used to feeling less than,
smarter than you about my lot in life.
I'm a professional nothing,
purposely passive,
unable to see the reason for my existence.
Why did you make me?
What is my meaning?
Who was I created to be?

Thank you for telling me what you really feel.
I love you as you are.
I hear your pain, confusion, discouragement,
your wavering want to try.
I value honesty more than trying to please,
for you can't please me more
than reaching out, taking the time to talk.
Listening however much you can
is enough for our communion.
You're only one step off the path for growth,
for meaning to your journey.

I'm always just ahead to lead you.
A teaspoon of trust

*is enough to move towards change
from comfortable chaos to calm.
Your purpose in life is to follow me,
and the rest, the best
will come when it's time.
You've enough love today to give it away
to someone with less than you.
My plan is share a smile with a stranger.
You have more peace than you know.
A piece will pass today from you
to someone poor of heart,
and you'll get back the grace
for one more step
toward healing, hope
and home.*

Joy

He said,

"JOY –
it doesn't get any better than this."

Me said,
"Oh my God…"

You rang?

You always answer when I ring.
Is that the same as
"Knock and the door shall be opened?"

Anyway you call, I come.

So why do I seek and don't find?
Joy is better than this,
but I've never found it all my life.

You found me, and I AM fill-in-the-blank.

Then why does my blank feel empty?
Why doesn't my hole heal?

It isn't time,
but you are in my perfect care.
You are the most precious
person in the world to me.

What about them?

They are, too.
I love them no less and no more than you,
but I provide uniquely for each life I've created.
And I am providing for you –
job or jobless,
without home, within mansion,
happily married or three times divorced.
I take care of all you need.

Feel better now? Not so depressed?

Sort of. What happened?

*We shared life and conversation;
we told the truth
and took time to weed out some lies
that grow in your heart
until all that grows in you is me.*

Is this joy?

It doesn't get any better than this.

I didn't know.

It was time.

Chapter 6

Learning To Wrestle

I believe that wrestling with God honors Him. That's why there are Biblical illustrations of it, like Abraham in Genesis 18 trying to convince God not to destroy Sodom and Gomorrah if there are 45 righteous men in the city. Or what about 20? Or 15? Or 10? God didn't seem to mind Abraham negotiating with Him.

Moses, however, found out that sometimes whining can irritate God. One day he was out in the wilderness, taking care of the family sheep when a bush burst into flame, but didn't burn up. God wanted to get his attention. God then told Moses to deliver the Israelites from their slavery in Egypt and lead them to a good land.

Moses' first assignment was to tell Pharaoh the Israelites were leaving. Moses was horrified at the idea, but God said not to worry about it, for He would be with him. Assignment number two was to tell the people of God's plan.

> *But Moses protested, "If I go to the people of Israel and tell them, 'The God of your ancestors has sent me to you,' they will ask me, 'What is his name?' Then what should I tell them?" God replied to Moses, "I AM WHO I AM. Say this to the people of Israel: I AM has sent me to you."* Exodus 3:13-14 (NLT)

God again told Moses to go, and He would make sure the people would believe His message. Apparently Moses wasn't paying attention.

> *But Moses protested again, "What if they won't believe me or*

> *listen to me? What if they say, 'The LORD never appeared to you'?"* Exodus 4:1 (NLT)

God showed Moses several miracles he could do to prove His point.

> *But Moses pleaded with the LORD, "O Lord, I'm not very good with words. I never have been, and I'm not now, even though you have spoken to me. I get tongue-tied, and my words get tangled."*
>
> *Then the LORD asked Moses, "Who makes a person's mouth? Who decides whether people speak or do not speak, hear or do not hear, see or do not see? Is it not I, the LORD? Now go! I will be with you as you speak, and I will instruct you in what to say."*
>
> *But Moses again pleaded, "Lord, please! Send anyone else."*
>
> *Then the LORD became angry with Moses. "All right," he said. "What about your brother, Aaron the Levite? I know he speaks well. And look! He is on his way to meet you now. He will be delighted to see you. Talk to him, and put the words in his mouth. I will be with both of you as you speak, and I will instruct you both in what to do.* Exodus 4:10-15 (NLT)

We *can* piss God off. Notice that Moses still didn't get out of his assignment. In wrestling with God, He can get mad at you, too. Honest talks with God go both ways. Your Uncensored Prayers not only honor God because you are trusting Him by telling the truth, but God honors *you* with the same respect. How 'bout that!

My husband Bud has a spotted history, much of it dreadful. God pulled a 180 on him, an act of redemption and the transforming power of God's love. Everyone who knew him was amazed and grateful.

Then God called Bud to be an ordained minister, because he was uniquely qualified to reach people with a similar background. Everyone who knew Bud was appalled or laughing hysterically, sure that God had lost His mind this time.

No one was more horrified than Bud. He and God fought about it for two years before anyone else knew but me. Bud kept telling God, "Ain't going there." God kept saying, *Oh yes you are. Those people need you, because they may not listen to anybody else but you about my acceptance and forgiveness.*

Then God said, *I want you to get a Master of Divinity degree.* Bud said, "Yeah right. Next you'll be telling me you want me to be a ballerina." God led Bud to a seminary by "accident" and arranged for tuition. He made all A's in his first semester, and can't wait for the next class to begin.

God grabbed an uncooperative man by the hair and didn't let go until the miracle happened and Bud said, "Yes." Wrestling is what it took. And wrestling with God is what it takes at times for each of us to prepare for the ministry God has specially planned. See why God likes to fight with us? It works.

Did you know wrestling with God is worship and glorifies Him? Shocking, isn't it. Jesus struggled with his calling, got exasperated with the disciples he had picked, and almost backed out about the crucifixion until he surrendered to his Father's will at the last minute.

If wrestling with God was good enough for Jesus...

This chapter is about the difficulty of learning to wrestle, not only with God, but also with ourselves. It's hard to face the truth that we love some sins and feel comfortable with behaviors that hurt ourselves and others because we're used to them, and change is always hard. God promises not only to wrestle with us through our issues, but He will also help us as we wrestle with ourselves.

The Hurt Healer

The ugly room is part of me,
saturated with pain,
pockmarked plaster scars of violent past energy.
My past bleeds into present stains
that painted smiles don't cover,
solid in concrete, lovely as faded beige.

Love it.

What?

It needs you.

It IS me.

No, it's trapped action, not identity.
It reminds you of ugly memories
you pick at 'til they bleed.

So it's my fault that I hurt?

Your choice to hold your past hostage
to the hilt with guilt.
But if you want, I'll help you accept it as is.
Love the pain to gain freedom
from the shame you claim as you, as your forever.
You have to love it to leave it
and buy some beauty with trust to try something new.

I don't trust me.

Trust ME, you goose.
You can't possibly pull this off.
I'm the hurt healer,
lover of lonely rooms that represent your life.

It's mine.

So give it to charity.
Dump it all on me – I can take it away,
leaving nothing but space to build your heart's desire.

Is this for real?

*Pick out the you you want
and we'll create your new life together,
a self you can enjoy and share without shame,
sanctuary at home in your heart.*

Damaged Trust

It hurts the worst
when the person I've hurt
is the one I love the most.
Excuses don't exist.

"I didn't mean to" doesn't count.
I can't promise nevermore
and "I'll try" seems so lame.

Trust is damaged, though love lasts.
There's hope, but I don't feel it.
Humiliation haunts me
and I wish there was somewhere
to hide from my shame.
The pain pervades my heart
and all my thoughts are dark.

Oh God, help me bear this through the night
and light a star for me.

Stark Dark

The black sack has found me
and tied me up within.
You said there is nowhere
your love can't reach.
It doesn't help.

I want you here with me in this sack
to hold me back to front,
arms around to keep the black at bay,
to stay where no one else can reach,
can find me in the stark dark
all around like ultrasound,
seeing the hidden deep inside.

Hide with me, hurt with me,
not for me.
I hate sympathy; empathy isn't deep enough.
But you are badder than shame,
gooder than kindness
with caring that cuts through any hell
to resurrect me from rigor mortis of my soul.
Keep me safe from my self-destruction,
and hug me whole again.

Halfly Committed To God

Again.
AAAARRRRGGGG!!!
The same ol' sin pulls me under one more time
and I know what the problem is –
I'm halfly committed to God,
three-fourths on a good day.
This is not conducive to victory.
Why can't I give in, give up,
give over this albatross to God?

I reckon this is the one thing He can't do.
I mean won't do.
How I wish He would do this for me –
surrender to surrender.

I'm religiously reluctant
and I know God doesn't honor religion.

He wants obedience,
which is like a four-letter word to me.
I want to, but that isn't good enough.
Being good doesn't cut it.
I want to let it go, let *me* go,
but I hate to admit that I love the sin more than God.

Yikes that hurts.
Sounds so egotistical (it is).
Being honest about this sucks.
What will it take?
I know He'll discipline me (another four-letter word)
because He loves me and I dread that.
I'm like a little kid, sneaking around
yet knowing that God sees all,
knows my ornery heart.
Sneaking around other people
(who probably know anyway)
doesn't make me feel any better.

But feelings don't have anything to do
with following Jesus.
Passing up peace

is obviously a price I'm willing to pay
and I'm not proud of being proud.
So what do I really want?
My way – permission to get all the benefits
while protecting my sin,
which ain't gonna happen.
I'm not OK about this
and I wouldn't want a God
who was OK with this, either.

The bottom line
is not wanting but *doing* –
doing what is in my best interest
because that's what God promises me.
My promises don't count and don't work.
Help, God, help!
No, in this case help yourself, fool,
to peace at any price –
freedom, loving God more than fill-in-the-blank.
Self, the only way to end this war is by surrender.
It's going to rub your fur backwards and hurt for awhile,
but you're worth it.

Let Me Lead

I never have to force your will, God,
and yet here I am,
trying to force the ugly stepsister's foot
into Cinderella's slipper.
I know I asked for your will,
know what happens when I take mine, but...

There are no 'buts' to my will.

I know, but...

You gotta pick, kiddo.
You believe I know what's best.
My plan brings only deep contentment.

I thought it looked so right, so perfect
and I wanted it so bad.

So what?
We both know your picker's broken.
Want another train wreck to prove it again?

No, but it's sad to walk away from good
when what I have is squirreled up,
hurting, harming, eating me away.

Makes sense.
You want to leave,
but your sense ain't gonna solve this,
not this time, not ever.

I wish you'd been through this.

I have – a million times
with you and them, and all the thems before.
I think I know what I'm doing better than you.

No questions there.
I just feel stranded,
straddled with a clinch in my gut
that will not go away.

Just don't you go away.

Where would I go?

*Into your cave of oneness under a rock
alone with your addled brain for counsel.
Where does that take you?*

To hell.

*Well, I'm in hell, too,
but you don't have to be.
Wait here with me.
Wait for me to lead,
to tell you what and when.
This isn't fun or free from anguish.
Trust me.*

My faith...

*Is big enough.
I gave you all you have to begin with,
all you need,
but you have to use it.
Plug your faith into me and I'll turn it on
and it will work for you
in this situation and every time.
Now let go of your logic
and let me lead.*

I can't do this.

*I know, but I can.
All you have to be is willing.*

I'm willing now...

That's all I need to help you.

I didn't think you needed anything.

*I need your cooperation,
not your help.
Will you trust me with this?*

Right now, but...

*Right now is all you have
and I have you.*

And I have you.

...*OK.*

Chapter 7

The No Fail Fall

When we get on the mat with God, He will not allow us to fall, except into His arms.

> *Like an eagle that stirs up its nest,*
> *That hovers over its young,*
>
> *He spread His wings and caught them,*
> *He carried them on His pinions.* Deuteronomy 32:11 (NASB)

There have been so many times I've fallen on my ass, usually due to my own stupidity. I've been a "fallen woman", have "fallen off the wagon" and have hit the dirt, wondering if I could get back up or even wanted to.

Every time, whether it was my fault or not, God picked me up and carried me until I could walk again on my own. He never blamed, but came, even when I didn't call.

Simon Peter is a perfect example of the No Fail Fall. The night before Christ's crucifixion, Peter vowed that even if everyone else abandoned him, he wouldn't. Jesus told him that before a rooster crowed the next morning, Simon would deny him three times.

After Christ's resurrection, he came looking for Simon, who was out fishing with some other disciples. When Simon saw it was the Lord standing on the shore, he jumped into the water and headed to Jesus, leaving his friends to bring in the boat. The group ate breakfast together, and then Jesus and Simon had a conversation alone.

> *When they had eaten, Jesus said to Simon Peter, Simon, son of John, do you love Me more than these [others do--with reasoning, intentional, spiritual devotion, as one loves the Father]? He said to Him, Yes, Lord, You know that I love You [that I have deep, instinctive, personal affection for You, as for a close friend]. He said to him, Feed My lambs.*
>
> *Again He said to him the second time, Simon, son of John, do you love Me [with reasoning, intentional, spiritual devotion, as one loves the Father]? He said to Him, Yes, Lord, You know that I love You [that I have a deep, instinctive, personal affection for You, as for a close friend]. He said to him, Shepherd (tend) My sheep.*
>
> *He said to him the third time, Simon, son of John, do you love Me [with a deep, instinctive, personal affection for Me, as for a close friend]? Peter was grieved (was saddened and hurt) that He should ask him the third time, Do you love Me? And he said to Him, Lord, You know everything; You know that I love You [that I have a deep, instinctive, personal affection for You, as for a close friend]. Jesus said to him, Feed My sheep. John 21: 15-17 (AMP)*

There are three Greek words used in the New Testament for three different kinds of love; in English we just use the word "love" to cover all three. The first Greek word for love is *agapao*, meaning the deep, spiritual love we have for God. The second word is *phileo*, which describes the love we have for a friend. The third word for love is *eros*, from which we get the word "erotic" (I think you can figure that one out).

I quoted the passage in John 21 from the Amplified Bible, even though its explanations of love are lengthy to make the conversation clear.

> *Jesus asked Simon, "Do you love me (as God)?" Simon said, "Yes Lord, you know I like you (as a friend)." Jesus asked a second time, "Simon, do you love me?" Again Simon said, "Lord, you know I like you." The third time Jesus asked,*

"Well, do you really like me?" and it broke Simon's heart. Yet he still continued to tell the truth, "You know I like you."

I imagine Simon felt he had screwed up so badly that Jesus wouldn't want him around anymore. You see, Simon really loved the Lord, and Jesus knew it. Simon was ideally suited to make a great church leader one day, because he knew personally the forgiveness, grace, and mercy of God, and it profoundly changed his life.

Simon engaged in the spiritual practice of wrestling with God. Even though he was ashamed, he was honest with Jesus, and because Jesus still wanted him on his crew, Simon was willing to follow him again.

When he falls, he will not be hurled headlong, because the LORD is the One who holds his hand. Psalm 37:24 (NASB)

The Lord upholds all those [of His own] who are falling and raises up all those who are bowed down. Psalm 145:14 (AMP)

Here's what I can say today with confidence:

Do not gloat over me, my enemies!
For though I fall, I will rise again.
Though I sit in darkness,
the LORD will be my light. Micah 7:8 (NLT)

Thanks be to God.

In this section, I explore the potential benefits of failure. God knows we are all going to fall sometimes, but He'll already be at the bottom to catch us. Sometimes we have to hit bottom to face truth. At that point, there are only two options: staying at the bottom, or crawling out the hole with God into the light of His redeeming love. God often lets His children fall without intervening so we can experience resurrection to a new life that would never happen with sudden salvation.

The Invasion of Insanity

My experience is in trusting the untrusty,
doubting what's real
in exchange for feelings of deliberate danger,
one silk thread from dead,
yet with every fragment of me
held by God who did not let me drop
nor stop my will to wander
and wallow in the worst,
because He wanted me
to want Him for love alone
to learn love is tough, but not cruel.

The seeming safety of lies
hurts worse than truth.
My right to rebel brought bondage, not freedom,
and the madness of God's mercy for me
invaded my insanity,
touched what I couldn't
and looked at me with kindness
until I could look back
and see my past for real,
then step over into today.

The Searing Truth

Pain is a waiting room
where everything's on fire,
but running just intensifies
the flaming desire to go to black.
Temporarily or dead stop,
trapped in front of closed doors,
I can breathe in the searing truth
that cremates lingering fantasies
or futilely fight to control a phantom
that doesn't mind.

Actually, the bigger the bad,
the less I resist –
succumbing to tranquility,
pain intact,
failing into the arms of God.

The No Fail Fall

The hardest part
in raising my young
isn't letting go,
but letting fall without rescuing,
allowing hurt without the Band-aid solution
that magically makes it all better, for now.

The dichotomy of this difficult act of love
is breaking my promise to always be there,
always help and protect,
allowing my kids the chance
to fly or fail, cope or crash,
flounder for now, or forever
so they have the chance in dark, in despair
to hit bottom and learn there is
a limit to falling, a point of return
and a God at the end of the load.

Resurrection

God could have prevented this,
intervened against evil.
I would have avoided agony and much loss,
such depression that the hole is dark,
deep, almost devoid of light left to see
any hope of rescue this time.
But what makes me think
that God chose this Thursday
to suddenly abandon me,
stop providing in spite of my predicament.

Could it be that He loves me enough
to leave me alone,
enduring the pain along with me,
suffers to lay aside sudden salvation
so I can gain strength from bearing my cross,
believing beyond circumstantial deprivation
to see the invisible restoration to come –
resurrection of life that cannot be achieved
without death and delay of Sunday's dawn.

Chapter 8
Daddy God

Abba means "daddy" in Aramaic, like a child would say. It's a very personal term that indicates the unquestionable trust a small child has in a parent. "Daddy" was Jesus' name for God in his Uncensored Prayers. In the Garden of Gethsemane, the day before he was crucified, Jesus was depressed and in great emotional pain. All his friends had let him down, and he knew the horrific ordeal awaiting him. Jesus wanted his Daddy, calling out to his "Abba" (Mark 14:36).

Daddy is the personal name we have the right to call God, because we have the same Daddy as Jesus. Isn't that astounding?

> *For you have not received a spirit of slavery leading to fear again, but you have received a spirit of adoption as sons by which we cry out, "Abba! Father!"* Romans 8:15 (NASB)

No matter how old we are, we long for the comfort of our parents.

A few years ago, my older brother and his family came to my house for the holidays. During the night, their grown son started throwing up. He woke up his mother for comfort and help. It didn't matter that he was an adult – he wanted his mama. Our heavenly parent is not only our Daddy, but also our Mama. Jesus said,

> *"Jerusalem, Jerusalem, who kills the prophets and stones those who are sent to her! How often I wanted to gather your children together, the way a hen gathers her chicks under her wings, and you were unwilling."* Matthew 23:37 (NASB)

Daddy God is also our protector.

> *He will cover you with his feathers, and under his wings you will find refuge; his faithfulness will be your shield and rampart.* Psalm 91:4 (NIV)

Did you know God your Father is proud of you? Here's what occurred when Jesus was baptized:

> *And a voice from heaven said, "You are my dearly loved Son, and you bring me great joy."* Luke 3:22 (NLT)

Another translation says,

> *"With you I am well pleased."* (NIV)

My earthly daddy is a retired pastor. Often when I was a child, he took me with him when he was invited to preach at another church. When daddy introduced me, he liked to say, "Joy is my favorite daughter." After a pause, he'd say, "Actually, she's my only daughter, but I'm proud of her, and wanted her to come with me today." Daddy wanted my company, and that made me feel so special. You're one of God's favorite children, too. We all are.

Daddy God wants our company, just like my daddy feels about me. Unfortunately, our human fathers aren't able to give us everything we need, but God can.

When my children were young, their father and I got a divorce. It was hard for me, but devastating for the children. There was a huge hole for them that no one else could fill. God inspired me to write a song for them that always made them cry, but they asked me to sing it over and over again. It was called, "You Are I AM". Our kids missed their daddy who was no longer there for them, who wasn't around when they wanted his help. I wanted them to know God was their Daddy who never left, and was able to perfectly meet their every need that only daddy's can provide.

> *Because you are sons, God has sent forth the Spirit of His Son into our hearts, crying, "Abba! Father!"* Galatians 4:6 (NASB)

Do you think of God as your Daddy? He feels that personal about you. Think about it.

In this chapter, I share some of my experiences with Daddy God. To recognize that God is our heavenly Daddy, we first must see ourselves as His children. He has adopted us into His family, so we have the same Daddy as Jesus. God honors our relationship with our earthly daddies, but Daddy God meets some of our deepest needs that our human daddies can't always provide. Daddy God is available to us every single minute, providing the comfort and protection every child wants, plus He's proud of us, even when we fail.

The No Fail Daddy

Do you hear it?

Doesn't matter.
In my toes and eyelashes
hums my hesitant reply and your persistent call.

I am here.

Then why the endless ache for that to matter?
Make enough serenity
to fill the gaping hole.

I always love you.

The thing I want the most
and fear to trust as true.

I'm your Daddy,
never leave you,
promise to take care of you.

But daddies fail to follow through.

Your faith is enough.

I believe, but balk
at falling fully into your embrace.

I won't make you.

Help me come.

I will give you rest.

I reach...

I trust you, child.

Please don't.
My best will disappoint.

I know, so I sent Jesus.

On the edge...are you out there?

I'm right here.
Ain't goin' nowhere.

You Are I AM

Is there a daddy who never leaves?
Is there a friend who always understands?
Is there a husband who can make me whole?

I AM, I AM, I AM, I AM.

Is there a parent who is always wise?
Is there a boss who is always fair?
Is there a brother who always wants me?

I AM, I AM, I AM, I AM.

Whatever you need, I AM the answer.
Wherever you go, I'm already there.
You can't offend me with the truth
or drive me away.
I'm not like any other;
I'm in you to stay.

I AM, I AM, I AM, I AM.

Is there a mother who can always help me?
Is there a doctor who can heal my heart?
Is there a pastor who is always right?

I AM, I AM, I AM, I AM.

Is there a friend who never breaks a promise?
Is there a leader who never lies?
Is there someone who understands me?

I AM, I AM, I AM, I AM.

I will accept you when you hurt me.
I will respect you when you're immature.
I'll never shame you when you fail
or turn you away.
I'm not like any other;
I'm in you to stay.

I AM, I AM, I AM, I AM.

You are the daddy who never leaves.
You are the friend who always understands.
You are the husband who can make me whole.
You are I AM, you are I AM.
You are the parent who is always wise.
You are the boss who is always fair.
You are the brother who always wants me.
You are I AM, you are I AM.

Indispensable

I am indispensable only to you, God.

Irreplaceable, irrecyclable, irritating and dear.
You're one of my favorite children.

I thought everybody was.

Well, yeah, but we're talking about you right now.
My universe wouldn't be complete without you.

That delights me and scares the bejeebers out of me.
I feel so small, so short next to your bigness.

The better to hold you with, my dear.
All I am surrounds you,
underneath you lifting up your cares, your prayers.
I know and honor you –
broken, mended strong and lively.
Living to love you – that I AM.

I haven't words to say...

For once.

how humble this makes me feel –
to know you love me this way, always, anyway I am.
I couldn't do that for anyone.

I haven't asked you to. I'm God, not you.
In the beginning, I created you just as you are,
just as I want you and I'm proud of you,
and show my friends your picture on the frig.
I tell the stars and trees how precious you are
and all creation dances.

Sending Jesus is the best thing I've ever done.
He went to bring you home,
wandering truant blindfolded to the truth.
You must be led to the light and loved into life.
Left alone, you're like a car with a bad wheel alignment;
you lurch into ditches without repair

that only I can give,
and what a joy that is for me.
Do you believe me?
...Are you still there?

I don't know how to say thank you sufficiently.
All I can do is praise you,
humble myself before your compassion and strength
and give myself to you.

That's all I want.

You're what I want.

What a splendid pair we are.

Pilgrim's Progress

Sometimes I wish you couldn't see me,
not because I want to hide,
but because I've ceased to try for awhile,
laid down my sword for junk food,
chosen cruise control over you.
Your faithfulness embarrasses me
when I'm silly, selfish and blind,
your kindness disregarded
and I don't care for anything
but a vacation from pilgrim's progress
to keep the faith.

Have a nice trip.
So where shall we go?

I want to be left alone.

Too late. I live inside you;
we're a package deal.
We zigzag life together
'til we end up at my house.

What the hell.

No, it's heaven.
Remember, you asked me in
so I take you wherever I go –
to bars and church, to bankruptcy
and back to love again.

I'm lost…

Yeah, but lost in love.
I take you as you are.

Today?

Forever. I don't renege because you do.

But I'm lazy…

So what's new.

I'm not trying today...

So why pray?
So why talk about what's true?
I'll be God, and you be you.
I value real even more than
you getting rewarded for righteousness.
This is part of the journey,
part of the deal
that I made with you to never leave.

You listen to so much crap from me.

But I also hear your heart
that never falters when you say you do.
You're not lying, but honest,
not humble, but hacking your way
back to the path.
Redemption is not a one-time event.
I multi-task with millions
of unreliable saints like you.

I'm an idiot. Sorry.

You're forgiven again.
Let's go rescue another fool
who will relate to you,
who needs to know my passion for people
isn't predicated on performance or patience
or strength to struggle all the time.
Get off your butt and do what you have to do.
I'll trail you just behind
until you let me lead again a little at a time.
You're my kid.

And you're my Daddy.

Thank heaven
for children
like you.

Chapter 9

Love And Acceptance

My daddy's ninetieth birthday was May 26, 2011. Over the last 30 plus years he's been the neighborhood grandpa, fixing bicycles and teaching kids all kinds of things. A number of years ago when he had a swimming pool installed in his backyard, one of the first things he did was teach my kids how to jump off the roof of the garage into the pool. My kids showed their friends how to do this, and they created variations that only teenagers would dare.

For daddy's eightieth birthday, he threw his own party and invited the church youth group over for hotdogs and swimming, promising to jump off the roof into the pool. Not only teens, but adults showed up with cameras to capture the event.

When daddy told mama he was really going to do this, she said, "But Jimmy, what if you hit the concrete instead of the pool?" His answer? "Well, there is that, but what a way to go!"

As my teenagers morphed into young adults, the parties got later and louder, with beer and cigarettes on hand. Daddy laid down some rules: turn down the music when we go to bed so the neighbors don't call the police, and clean up after yourselves when you leave. Remember this is a conservative retired preacher we're talking about. What was going on here?

Love and respect. He loves and accepts those kids as they are, and they've responded with love and respect for him and his very reasonable requests. Daddy has created a safe haven for them to hang out. They know my dad is a Christian, but he never preaches to them about anything. Those young people may not realize it, but they're seeing Jesus in my daddy. Many of them would never dream of going to church, so daddy has church in his swimming pool, teaching about the love of Jesus through how he lives.

Here is the text of daddy's living sermon:

> *We love, because He first loved us. 1 John 4:19 (NASB)*

He passes along what God has given him.

Often unspoken, sometimes verbally, daddy lets these kids know what God is like:

> *I have loved you with an everlasting love; I have drawn you with unfailing kindness. Jeremiah 31:3 (NIV)*

Believing that God loves and accepts us as we are carries a lot of validity when we live it out ourselves. And it all starts with God.

One of the most personal passages of Scripture for me never fails to choke me up, because it says God sees us as precious, honored and loved.

> *But now, thus says the LORD, your Creator, O Jacob,*
> *And He who formed you, O Israel,*
> *"Do not fear, for I have redeemed you;*
> *I have called you by name; you are Mine!*
> *When you pass through the waters, I will be with you;*
> *And through the rivers, they will not overflow you*
>
> *When you walk through the fire, you will not be scorched,*
> *Nor will the flame burn you,*
>
> *Since you are precious in My sight,*
> *Since **you are honored and I love you.**" Isaiah 43:1-2, 4 (NASB)*

God not only **loves us**, which is huge, but He **honors us**. What causes our Holy God to feel this way about us? I think He can't help it. It's how He's wired. Besides that, He chooses to feel and act that way. It's His nature, not ours, but He plants as much of His nature into us as we want and are capable of comprehending.

As I've struggled about my love and acceptance issues with God, He's taught me as much as I can understand how to first love and accept myself, then I can show it to others by how I live. Sometimes I can actually do that (!!!), but I keep practicing, like I practice Uncensored Prayer. The more I hang around God, the more His love and acceptance ends up in me, and I find it leaking out to those around me. Just like God, I can't help it.

In this section I address something we all want but don't always get: to be treated with respect and dignity. We can't give to others what we don't already possess, and many of us have trouble loving and accepting ourselves. This is something I struggle with personally. A sense of worthiness comes from God, who calls us worthy. He honors us unconditionally because He loves us as we are. When we believe this truth, we become capable of loving and accepting ourselves, gaining the capacity to offer it to other people, too.

The Radical Artist

Words usually work,
but you're an unusual God
and I'm still unused to your grace,
your face appearing on trees
in lacy spider webs,
collective clouds even in my mind.
You made me as I am
and love me this way.
I still don't get it
and wonder that you want to.

When we talk, you listen
and I hear you with my heart
and from other people
tuned to you, whether they know it or not.

You use the weirdest ways to capture me,
reel me to you, hooked by your love
for life – past and future – but especially today
where I breathe and try to fathom your plan
that I just barely understand.
Your directions are simple
but I still feel overwhelmed,
screaming "I can't handle this!"
You wait until I relax and surrender what I can,
and when I step into the scary, you hold my hand
like a toddler, wobbling with you into the wild.

Creation is always radical,
coloring without lines to define the unknown.
The established resists
as if invaded by a dangerous foe –
be it second-born sibling
or alternate point-of-view.
Ever the new seems to threaten the now,
challenging what we know
with the unnamed.

God will not be tamed into duplicate-making;
identical twins come with souls of their own.
Beauty and genius are just as maligned

as wretched deformity.
Lacking conventional needs to conform,
the artist is always at odds with the average,
risking rejection to realign truth
into Polaroid pictures of God.

A Crutch For Now

Poor little crippled child,
halting steps in steeled attempts
to be invisible amidst furtive eyes.
Those who try to gawk unnoticed
only underline the truth,
undermining precious worth
of one who can't help how they are.
I know this pain too well,
as different from the nicer norm
as a bum at a ball instead of a bar.
I cling to my crutch for safety,
insurance from a fall into embarrassed fear,
unwanted exposure of inadequacy above all.

What about acceptance?

Yeah right...and I'm the queen of England.

Possibly.

I want to be normal.

Really? Mediocre?
Cookie-cutter made like someone else
made like someone else et al.?
I created you unique, a creative skill of mine I love
as I love you the way you are.

But what of the crutch?
It means I'm lame and weak,
unable to stand tall before you,
proud to be someone you're proud of,
tossing the crutch to lean on you.

If that never happens, I love you
and I'm proud of how you're made –
not just hair and spleen, but crippled.

Oh no...

Oh yes I do.

*Love yourself enough
to use your crutch until it falls away
and I'll be here, no matter what,
because you matter to me.*

Unconditional Love

Unconditional love is acceptance
as is, as was,
embracing the beauty
and the least easy to honor with equal grace,
granting myself the right to desires
that cannot be willed or forced into real,
but choosing to challenge the easier path
of petty pleasures devoid of gain
with the pain of secret sacrifice
sweetened by love's unfailing irony –
the giver gets the gift.

Liking Before Love

I've not always been the prodigal child.
When I was short, there were a few years
when I believed I was completely safe
until abuse struck savagely
and blew that all away.
It was up to me to protect myself,
and since I couldn't do that,
I was lost for life,
out there on my own alone,
branded for worse, not better.

Yes, better times occurred
(angels must have worked over-time to pull that off).
I fell into the Grand Canyon on a regular basis,
escaping on trains that often wrecked,
recovering until it happened again,
always my fault, I thought.
And yet I survived,
knowing God had something to do with that.
Why? Why him?

Significant mothers failed the comfort test;
partners never made me whole.
I excelled at sabotaging success
from fear I couldn't achieve,
failed to self-destruct
for fear of damning judgment on the other side.

And yet…
and yet…
I've always had enough hope to keep trying,
lying as a shield from certain abandonment,
craving as my deepest wound
to be wanted and loved as was, is, gonna be.
"Nothing is impossible with God"
didn't mean he would do anything for me.
Have I mentioned fear,
the premier power in my soul?

So how did I transform to here?
Better at balance

though sometimes still insane,
warped and eccentric but cursed no longer
than a temporary choice.
I think I got the deal that God likes me,
which was more important to accept than love.

I've heard a hundred times
that love is a decision, not an emotion,
but liking someone means commonalty,
contented and being comfortable with each other
without the pact of commitment
that can stay held together by legal glue.

But God liking me had to come before love
for me to trust again.
Several people very important to me
have said, "I love you, but...,"
"You did a great job, but..."
The most significant thing God ever gave me
was "I like you. Period,"
which I had to believe as real for me
before I could ever accept
God's "I love you. Period. The End."

He and I are best friends now
and I'm not afraid to say what I really think to him,
even when I'm FUBAR as hell,
because it makes him smile when I'm honest.
Knowing he accepts me
makes it possible for me to hear anything he says.
God knows if he lectures me, I'm history,
but I've learned he meets me where I am
and makes a big deal over baby steps.

When a major epiphany occurs,
God jumps in with all eighty-zillion feet
to honor my lunge of faith,
and I'm exhilarated to understand
a blast of truth that doesn't go away.

I've learned it's OK to learn what I can
and not be trashed by C- scores,
because I'm valuable for who I am, as I am

and progress will happen from here.
Retro responses don't mean it's all over anymore,
even when doubt is louder than faith
because I finally know God believes in me,
not because he can,
but wants to, wants me
and forward isn't a fraud.

Chapter 10

Helping Others

It's still easy for me to fall into old behavior and feel I need help more than I need to help others. Several periods in my life the version of my "personal" Bible read, "Give, and it will be taken from you." Thank God for friends who refused to put up with that schlock. When I chose only to take, they gave anyway. Over time, they gently refused to let me just take. Literal victimhood didn't have to be a permanent way of life. Only by learning to help other people did I learn to help myself.

Once I became willing to trust another hurting person with my own story of pain, I discovered how much we needed each other, to share the burden, the shame of feeling different and damaged. It had never occurred to me that someone might grab my shirt and say, "Where have you been? I thought I was the only one." Little did they know I thought the same thing about them.

Isolation is both a protection and a curse. Alone, with just my mind for company, I perceive the world as more dangerous than it is. No one can be trusted with the truth. I become my own sorry savior, "safe" only when isolated. Sometimes desperate loneliness is the only thing that will make us reach out to another, or allow someone in who reaches out to us.

I was afraid that if I set aside my own needs to help someone else, the hole left in me would be empty forever. Giving all I had would leave me destitute, which is what God wanted, right? I mean, look at the Bible story of the poor woman giving her offering at the temple:

> *LOOKING UP, [Jesus] saw the rich people putting their gifts*

Helping Others 133

into the treasury.

And He saw also a poor widow putting in two mites (copper coins).

And He said, Truly I say to you, this poor widow has put in more than all of them;

For they all gave out of their abundance (their surplus); but she has contributed out of her lack and her want, putting in all that she had on which to live. Luke 21:1-4 (AMP)

To please God, I had to give everything I had, leaving me nothing. That woman had to starve to death to please God. Like I was going to agree to that. I don't think so. Go find another sucker to please you, God.

It didn't occur to me that the passage in Luke wasn't the end of the widow's story:

And my God will meet all your needs according to the riches of his glory in Christ Jesus. Philippians 4:19 (NIV)

That verse applies to all of us, even me (I tend to be God's exception, you know). It took awhile for God to eradicate that entrenched belief in me. Here's how He did it.

God told me He had no intention of helping me right then. If I wanted my need for understanding and comfort to be met, I was going to have to get it from someone. God was going to put a hurting person in my path who would relate to me if I was willing to tell them about myself. I would have to be honest, perhaps with a complete stranger, about my painful past and current faults and fears. That person would relate to my experience in life, and I would relate to theirs. *Then* God would jump in with a miracle, providing what we need.

*Two people are better off than one, for they can help each other succeed. If one person falls, the other can reach out and help. But **someone who falls alone is in real trouble**. Ecclesiastes 4:9-10 (NLT)*

I knew plenty about the "trouble" part. Now I began to experience the blessing of helping someone else. Not everyone to whom I extend friendship wants it; there is neither gratitude nor response for some acts of grace. But every act of kindness comes back around eventually.

> *A man reaps what he sows. Galatians 6:7 (NIV)*

Another translation says,

> *You will always harvest what you plant. Galatians 6:7 (NLT)*

Believe me, I'm very inconsistent about giving as a way of life. I'm a loner by nature and prefer to stay at home, surrounded by books and family. I'm much more comfortable praying for someone rather than getting out and doing something tangible. Here's the cattle prod for me:

> *For just as the body without the spirit is dead, so also faith without works is dead. James 2:26 (NASB)*

Now I share honestly about my life and my personal experience of practicing Uncensored Prayer through wrestling with God. For a loner, this has required courage I don't naturally have, trusting God's promise to give me what I need. Through this book, my prayer is God will enable you to make the commitment to practice Uncensored Prayer, then pass your experience to others who would benefit from it, too.

God says, *"You want me to believe you're committed to me? Prove it. Follow me, which involves getting involved with people. There's the door. Are you coming?"*

This chapter deals with our need to both give and receive. Everyone wants to be needed by someone. God created us to need each other. No one is complete by themselves. When we give from the heart of God within us, the gift is returned multiplied, whether the recipient cares or not. But also God places certain people in our path who can only find their way home to God through us. We aren't God, but to these people, we are the messengers of His salvation, and in helping them, we find the help we need.

The Specialist

Buried beneath a billion doctors,
millions of surgeons, specialists,
herbalists, chiropractors,
there's a handful
of critical burn surgeons for hands –
people who puzzle-piece
skin back together,
fight infection
with the victims of fire, explosions,
trauma to bodies fighting for life.
They save a small sub-group of people
and give their best to the patients who die.
They're irrelevant to those who don't have the need,
irreplaceable when it's you.

And most of the time I feel I don't matter.
My life consists of ordinary and odd
daily necessities and occasional bright bits of light
that help me continue one more day.
God, how boring, how blasé
to you and me both.
That's not all there is,
but it's all I have, all I know
of some meaningful purpose in life
that would make a difference to me.

But I was ambushed by a surprise today
that I hope and doubt might be actually true –
there's a sub-group of people or maybe just one
who needs a specialist, who needs me
because of my education in life,
because of my knowledge of life and death.

My experience uniquely qualifies me
to offer hope for their trauma and pain
'cause I've been there or live there
and manage to cope,
regardless of how other folk perceive me.
To the living dead, I'm their hope for help
and if they don't find me
they may not make it, may not survive

the burns to their soul.

Whether or not I believe this,
it matters to them –
someone who's a specialist
in their form of pain.
I can choose to remain
in my walled up world
or help heal that person with hope.
It's my choice, my calling by God
and it's my chance to matter
to me.

Needing Each Other

Lost doesn't mean I'm a loser.
I've been permanently found by God
and he never lets go and I never give up on him.
I've always lost and won at the same time,
wishing I could just be one or the other.
That's never been my lot in life
and today I think that's how I was created.

I may be wrong about this,
but God keeps putting people in my life
whom I understand
and who, upon hearing a little of my story, say
"Where have you been?
I thought I was the only one."
I've known that hell most of my life,
a closeness with God and a life out there.

A long time ago,
I watched men in outer space on TV –
all in the ship but one brave or stupid astronaut
floating outside in the dark
with only a fragile umbilical lifeline
keeping him from death.
And I knew that's me –
all the thems are in and I'm out,
floating without companionship,
not understood and solo
except for a solo Christ like me.
I don't understand his Godness,
but I never would have made it
without our mutual identification.

We need each other –
me to know love as is,
God to reach people who would never make it home
without my personal experience with life.
I'm too un-pious to draw a crowd,
but God brings them to me, one by one.
I never solve their problems or mentor them;
that's others' call in life.

My worth doesn't come from serving God,
following the Father faithfully,
but oh how humble and special I feel
when God performs a miracle and lets me be his partner,
when I see light in despairing eyes,
remembering last week when that was me.

I've heard so many public proclamations
of deliverance years ago
from drugs, divorce, and prison,
healed and reclaimed to a holier life.
I can't compete with that;
it isn't the real me,
but my little magnet draws those on the floor,
dropped by God in my direction.
He doesn't deal in quotas;
callings aren't like that in the Body of Christ.
No one chooses their role
but heads can't exist without livers,
both the vulnerably visible
and hidden unglamorous parts.

We need God and each other;
it's planned this way.
I can't understand God's choice in that,
but I believe what I see
and he uses me when least expected
to help both me and another at the same time –
a partnership both holy and human.

Giving What I Need

I don't care about Christmas anymore.
It seems so sad and empty,
something to do and be done with.
I refuse to just "buy something" for the people I love.
There is a special satisfaction in finding a gift
perfect for a precious someone,
and I would be lynched if I didn't fill
my tall kids' stockings with silly dollar store toys and kiddy candy
appropriate only for six-year-olds.
I really like that part,
but the carols, trees and seasonal scenes
have lost me, left me out to lunch.

To all the people glowing with delight,
asking if my shopping is complete
then interrupting with their answer
before hearing mine,
I just smile and give the expected response:
"Yes. Merry Christmas."
What else is there to say that's socially acceptable?

I just buried my dog with stomach cancer,
which doesn't help, but that's not what's wrong.
The lights at night are pretty but pointless,
poinsettias, packages,
pain my hurting heart can't celebrate,
and I don't even miss it,
but I don't have to explain this to you.

When you rode into Jerusalem
and the crowds welcomed you with joy,
I doubt that happiness filled your heart.
Grief and dread were primary
because you knew what was coming,
but I bet you smiled and waved anyway
because you loved them.
It was more important
to give them what they wanted
instead of what you did.

Is that the perfect gift I can give this year

to the people I care about?
What they want from me isn't my depression.
Help me give the gift you gave,
pocketing your needs to feed the hearts of others,
celebrating their joy.
So my candle isn't lit;
I can still light up their faces
with traditions that matter to them.

But I'm sick of faking it;
continuing will only make things worse.
I can't do this by myself.
Grant me the gumption
to feel for real what they need
and act on it with faith
that you will meet my needs, too.

The Gift of Grace

Courage to care is there
in tremulous tiny touches
of grace to the graceless,
even from me to me.
Sometimes it takes all God's strength
to wrest me away from myself long enough
to see someone else's lack of life,
to recognize the hope I have
in God who creates change
in anyone willing to give him a chance,
a try at anything better than our lousy best.

I have known the power of "Yes" to God,
of his willingness to grab my guilt
and lift me out of despair
when I feel I have nothing to give
to another heart hurting like hell for hope.
He readjusts my eyes to see the sight
of someone outside of me
who needs my tale of tears
and uneven journey given meaning
only by God's forgiveness,
faithful support to change course forever,
no matter what, without knowing how.

I am most effective at sharing God's love
when I don't pretty up my past,
don't deny my faults or faith or fears,
but let myself be real.
For then a real God can really reach
someone who doesn't believe in him
or themselves enough to understand
an outrageous story of God in skin
who died to set us free.

So many times I keep from telling this truth
because it sounds ridiculous
and I don't know how to make it make sense
to anyone but me.
But when I try anyway,
God intervenes and interprets what I say

to the one who is ready to receive.
And then a miracle happens –
truth and trust converge together
and both of us believe;
faith is passed as fire to fuel
and one more candle flames.

Chapter 11

God Is My Co-Author

I'm a radical writer. I know it. Basically, I write what comes up out of a careful thought process. But I'm also keenly aware that I only write well when inspired by God. Wait a minute – that sounds like how the authors of the Bible wrote.

> *All scripture is inspired by God. 2 Timothy 3:16 (NASB)*

Do I think I'm writing Scripture? Not at all. But all creative talent is given by God, though we have to cultivate it. He is the ultimate Creator, and gives us part of Himself for all of us to be creative.

> *I have filled him with the Spirit of God in wisdom,*
> *in understanding, in knowledge, and in all kinds of*
> *craftsmanship. Exodus 31:3 (NASB)*

I write one of two ways. When God is my co-author, writing is a joy, even electric. I get alone, very still, and listen with my heart. It makes me think of a space observatory on an isolated hill in California with sensitive equipment listening to the sounds of the universe (and Martians, maybe).

Then there are times when I get this great idea and try to write by myself. It's like trying to pull a thought out of concrete. The result is difficult and awful, and ends up in the trash instead of my computer. Even though I know the results are always disastrous, I still try to write this way occasionally (I'm on a slow learning curve in this area). I think that since God is the giver of creative skill, a work of beauty is only achieved when He is involved.

The plan God has for our lives is a work of beauty that is fully realized when we partner with Him. It takes commitment and faith to follow the dream God has placed in our hearts, but we don't have to be brave, just willing. Even if you know what you want to be when you grow up, or you are already living out that plan, God will always drag us out of our comfort zone if we follow Him. Nothing safe is exciting. Nothing easy is fulfilling. The only thing we can count on God to do is keep His promises. Everything else God does is original, personal, and unexpected.

When Jesus picked the twelve disciples to take his Followers 101 class, they made a commitment to follow him – literally – because he was always going somewhere. They didn't know it at the time, but they had signed up for a three year tour of duty. At the end, only one didn't re-enlist – that's the impact Jesus had on their lives.

Living with Jesus changes us, just like it did for the original twelve. When we learn to trust God intimately with our feelings and thoughts, He reveals His plan for our lives, which might be what we've always longed for. Then again, it might be the very last thing we could imagine doing. Trusting God to go with Him wherever that leads, doing whatever than means, will be based on mutual love. Look what will happen:

> *Take delight in the LORD, and he will give you the desires of your heart. Psalm 37:4 (NIV)*

God's desires become our desires, and our commitment to Him will result in this:

> ***Commit*** *your way to the LORD,*
> *Trust also in Him, and He will do it. Psalm 37:5 (NASB).*

God will do what? Help us keep our **commitments**. He knows the temptation to slack off, cut corners, and flat-out quit.

Here's another promise God makes to help us:

> *Commit to the LORD whatever you do, and he will **establish** your plans. Proverbs 16:3 (NIV)*

"**Establish**" means to make it happen. It means to make the dream come true.

Commitment usually involves something long term, through success and failure, doubt and hope. Somewhere in there, fear will eclipse faith, but by talking it out with God, love can conquer fear, and faith will be restored. Jesus said,

> *All things are possible to him that believes. Mark 9:23*
> *(NASB)*

But my faith in God (and me) to pull this off wavers sometimes. Fortunately, God already thought of that and has an answer to the problem.

> *If you have faith the size of a mustard seed, you will say to this mountain, "Move from here to there," and it will move; and nothing will be impossible to you. Matthew 17:20*
> *(NASB)*

God says when I have bite-size faith, it's enough. And that's enough for me, until the next time fear reappears. But this time I know if I wrestle it out with God, love can conquer fear, and faith will be restored.

In this chapter, I reveal the conflicts that I have experienced from following God's call for me to be an author. None of us are created by chance. Each of us have a unique place in God's universe, made in His image to fulfill a special part of His plan for the redemption of all of us. When we are willing to listen to Him, God will disclose His purpose for our lives – something we cannot do by ourselves, but which God enables us to fulfill, whether it be an innate talent we already possess, or an ability God creates from scratch, so He gets the glory, not due to our inherent gifts, but because God has made us partners in His plan for the restoration of all His creation. The individual challenge is daunting; the benefits are extraordinary.

Creative Collaboration

Caught in my throat,
the words won't come up or out,
whispered or shouted,
cramped in my hand.

Do you understand?
You spoke life into life.
Did I stick in your throat
when you called my name?

I'm ashamed to admit this,
but you already know
the whole point's ludicrous.

I mean, I'm writing this,
but I've been on pause in heart hibernation,
unable to everything you've gifted me to be.

Perhaps you've waited for me to
want again our partnered words.
For made in your image,
we work best together,
creative confidence
that spills out whole from our soul –
your love and my cooperation,
collaborative renaissance
you intend for me.

Hate Mail

You know I'm going to get a lot of hate mail
from some people when I come out,
when I go public about you and me.

You ought to read MY hate mail.

I cower under criticism, and the rabid kind…
I'm not up to that.
You can slough it off, but I can't.

You think it doesn't hurt me?
It tears me up when people I love don't love me back.
I give them the best I've got
and I just want to help them,
but they think I'm terrible,
out to get them, or don't even exist.

How do you take the abuse?

Well, I'm God. I absorb their anger,
forgive them, and let it go.

I can't do that.
It's so easy to say, "Let go and let God,"
but that feels like letting go of you
and there's no way I'm going to do that,
because you're the only hope I have
of making it through this.
But I'm afraid your help won't be enough.
I hate to say it, but I don't trust you that much.

Have I ever asked you to be something you're not?

I don't think so.

Your fears are real and valid.

I know you're with me and are reliable, but…

But what?

I'm afraid to find out. What if…

I leave you stranded to test your faith?
What kind of God do you think I am?

I'm scared shitless…

but not Godless.
You don't have to be brave to follow me.

You are out of your mind.
If I follow the plan you've given me,
it'll be the bravest thing I've ever done.

Where's this 'if' coming from?
Are you cancelling your commitment?
You can, you know.

Well, I've thought about it,
but mainly I'm worried about it.

Of course you are.
It's crazy to follow my plans.

Are you making fun of me?

Never. It makes no sense to follow a plan
that makes no sense to you.
This is where faith has to come into play.
Don't let fear of the pain that will inevitably come
keep you from living out your heart's passion.
It's time for your dream to come true,
and that's why I've called you now.
Yes, it's going to be difficult
and require every atom you have,
but I'm going to give you all I have.

I don't know if that's enough.

I AM enough, and together, so are you.

Commitment Crisis

You're breaking my heart.
I can't keep my end of the deal
on commitment to follow you.
You've asked too much of me.
That time I had the courage to say "Yes" was impulsive.
I wanted so bad to feel important
that I thought…just maybe…
your great idea would work.

I've never allowed myself to fully feel my dream
because it would hurt too bad
to hope for what I couldn't have.
And now I've gone and done it:
let myself believe my deepest heart's desire
would come true,
that what I've always wished I could be and do in life
was actually happening, and now I regret it.
I knew better and stepped outside my defensive wall
that has at least protected me
from unfixable disappointment and grief I can't bear.

God, I hurt so bad.
I don't think you lied to me,
but I lied to me in taking an unthinkable risk
to accept your plan for my passion.
You promised to help me
openly share my gift of words,
setting them free to end up in unknown hands.
You said if only one person made it home to you
because of me, my life was a success.

I know that's your priority, but it isn't mine.
I know that's selfish, but it's true.
What I really want
is to have many people read my work
and be deeply affected by someone else
who knows desperate despair,
yet shares a real, un-pretty relationship with God
who honors honesty and loves as is.

Uncensored Prayer

You always come where I am
and take me where I can't,
but what bothers me is I know you won't do my part
and my part is falling apart.
I made a commitment I can't keep.

Fear is eclipsing faith again
and I don't trust me to stand my ground.
I don't know...
I just don't know if I can step again
into my doubt with shaky hope
of looking through the window
to see if my dream reaches back at me.

Commitment isn't trying, but doing –
no matter what,
and I'm afraid I've failed already
because I'm scarred and scared.
I haven't retreated yet,
but I can't forward...
lost in limbo, not back to point one,
but pathless in an off-the-road truck
muddin' without joy.

Heart Hope

Listen to your heart, not your fear.
The heart hears hope
while fear tells lies,
sees spies in even faithful friends
who care enough to ask the second time
how you really are behind the social "Fine,"
whereas heart will help you know the truth
and bear it, if it causes pain,
sustains through boredom and defeat
and lasts to love in spite of fear
that "ifs" and "shoulds" and questions faith,
believing only in disaster,
scoffs at intuition and invalidates experience.

But heart knows what it knows
without need to prove or understand.
When honored, it will tell us
who we are and what we need;
when followed, it will take us home
nose to the ground,
tracking the unseen sacred path
unique to every soul
undeterred by howling in the dark
from terrors without teeth.

Co-Author With God

You brought life to life with words,
and I bring life to words with you,
co-authors on the page,
fully powerful when spoken
as music alone can open
certain chambers of the heart
to hear truth no other way.
And what I write always surprises me.
Unsought phrases sing and I follow,
listening, writing what I hear,
not as a copying scribe, but a wordsmith
giving the gift you gave me freedom to rise,
to reach beyond my wisdom
to create beauty out of pain.

It's not the same when I try it on my own.
Cheap imitations are obvious
pictures of fire lacking spark,
and the bigger I try the badder it gets
'til I torch the task for good.
For true inspiration always comes unbidden;
unannounced it appears in a single line
that grabs my attention and says "Follow."
If I say "Later," it leaves for good,
the line ending in a cul-de-sac,
but I'm rarely "Later" now.

For journeys with God are wild and original
along mapless tracks he made.
His ecstatic face glows in the light
for someone who wants to see,
and I'm compelled to go
where I don't know what will happen,
but free from failure.
For my own light writes without effort
thoughts I never would have planned
until the final word says "Finished"
and wonder comes anew.
For the first-draft baby is whole,
needing a few stray hairs tucked into place.

It's all me and all God,
this truth I need
meant for other me's out there
who believe no one knows
their own bleak blandness.
My words blow them out of hiding
yelling, "Where have you been?"
to both God and me,
as I've called the same for years.

The most successful lie Satan told me was,
"Who would want your work?
Who would read it – maybe ten?
Who would publish it, sell it,
tell it to friends?
We both know it's good, but it's meant for you,
so keep it safely home."
And I've believed,
because I couldn't see any alternative.

But God butted in right on his time and said,

Follow and bring your words.
It's time to give what you have for healing.
I'm your agent, tour guide;
leave it to me and you keep to the itinerary.

And my words said,
"It's nice to be out of the house;
I've always wanted to travel."

Chapter 12

Quitting The Quitting

Two very different men have had the most influence on my life, ingrained in childhood. They both preached love, but practiced it in opposite ways. Daddy loved me with an everlasting, unconditional love, emulating God. My abuser taught me that love meant slavery, pain, and lies. I simultaneously followed both their teachings, with disastrous results, as you can well imagine.

God tends to do things upside down and backwards from human ways. He worked His promise for my life in a most unlikely way:

> *God causes all things to work together for good to those who love God, to those who are called according to His purpose.*
> *Romans 8:28 (NASB)*

God allowed me to wander around and around in the wilderness for the first 40 plus years of my life before following Him into the Promised Land, because that's what it took for me. I persisted in making the same disastrous decisions with the same horrific results until I caught the drift that this wasn't working for me. I wasn't stupid, folks – just well taught.

I had been practicing perseverance. All good things can be transformed into weapons of mass destruction, depending on how they're used. When I finally became interested in spending time with God and pursuing Him through life, He used what I already knew about perseverance as a positive asset for me

There was a very important role (among many others) God played in those first years of my life. While I was the Coyote chasing the Road Runner with

Quitting The Quitting 155

predictable results, God supported me like Aaron and Hur did for Moses, because I couldn't do it for myself.

I have an affinity for trees. And developing a sense of perseverance is a lot like being a tree. It's not so much that they are often big and strong. It's about something they *don't* do.

I live in a part of the country full of deciduous trees, like oak and maple. In the fall, their leaves turn glorious colors and gradually fall off, replaced by new green leaves in spring. Often when I look at these trees in the winter, I think about their great faith in God. They drop their leaves in the fall, not their branches. If there were no branches in the spring, there would be no leaves, and the trees would die. All through the winter they lie dormant, sort of asleep, like bears hibernating. Weeks and months go by, and then it gets warmer, and here come the leaves.

Perseverance is like that, hanging in there during long tough times. Or when disasters come in herds. Or when the same weakness pulls us down for the zillionth time. God promises to help.

> *Fear not [there is nothing to fear], for I am with you; do not look around you in terror and be dismayed, for I am your God.* **I will strengthen and harden you to difficulties, yes, I will help you**; *yes, I will hold you up and retain you with My [victorious] right hand of rightness and justice. Isaiah 41:10 (AMP)*

> *He gives strength to the weary and increases the power of the weak. Isaiah 40:29 (NIV)*

That's God's part. Our part is quitting the quitting. It's learning to stop giving up on God when it's hard, to never give up even when everything suggests we should.

> *Therefore, since we are surrounded by such a great cloud of witnesses, let us throw off everything that hinders and the sin that so easily entangles. And let us run with* **perseverance** *the race marked out for us, fixing our eyes on Jesus, the pioneer and perfecter of faith. For the joy set before him he endured*

> *the cross, scorning its shame, and sat down at the right hand of the throne of God. Consider him who endured such opposition from sinners, so that **you will not grow weary and lose heart**.* Hebrews 12:1-3 (NIV)

Making the effort to try again every time we're down takes hope that things are going to get better. God provides that, too.

> *And not only this, but we also exult in our tribulations, knowing that tribulation brings about perseverance;*
>
> *and perseverance, proven character; and proven character, hope;*
>
> *and hope does not disappoint, because the love of God has been poured out within our hearts through the Holy Spirit who was given to us.* Romans 5:3-5 (NASB)

Devotedly pursuing anything – even destructive behavior – makes us faithful to the practice. The same principle is true in our relationship with God. Consistent wrestling with God requires faith that this will achieve something we desperately want: to matter, to succeed rather than fail, and to gain joy instead of junk.

Even when we fall into sin again, God honors even the weakest attempt to come back to Him, crawling out of the ditch onto the faith path once more – quitting the quitting. God rewards the simplest touch of faith, because it shows commitment to His infallible commitment to us.

The next time you give in, don't give up. I'm telling you this because I need to hear it myself.

Remember to keep your branches up when all your leaves fall off.

This section proposes there is a difference between repetitive sin and the belief that our situation is hopeless, that things will never change. It's true that our best efforts are ineffectual, but we can believe the lie that the way things are is permanent, and all we can do it accept it and muddle on. When we are willing to listen to God, He confronts us with our BS without blaming us, but without a quick-fix on our behalf. God will not do what we don't want. We have to be willing for Him to transform our lives, and when that happens, God engages all His power, predicated on our desire to change, to *be* changed, so that hope transcends despair.

Trying Again

I don't fall like leaves,
but like a basketball.
You're always there to pick me up,
even if my team doesn't.
Don't you have anything else to do?

Not more important.
I can really multi-task.
The best thing is you always get up and try again.

Don't my falls embarrass you?

I'm not people, kiddo.
Compassion is my middle name.

"Lord Compassion God"…I like that.

And I like you.
It takes gumption not to quit.
You may grumble, even pout,
but you don't lie down and play dead.

I don't see the point of that.
It doesn't solve anything.
Actually, I don't solve anything.
You're the puzzle pro and tell me the answers.

You don't always listen
until your solutions don't work.

But at least I know where to go.

That makes you faithful to me.
So many people don't even try that.
They don't know I'm the answer to their problems.

Took me a lot of trial and error (heavy on the error)
to figure that out.

But you did, and I'm proud of you.

And I'm proud of you.

We're one heck of a team.

Ain't it grand!

Failure in Perspective

Failure is the hole,
not the whole –
a flaw in the fabric,
a wound in the weave
that tends to bleed all over the colors
that celebrate the common success,
as if balancing the checkbook
doesn't count compared to smoking a cigarette
after quitting a zillion times.
My life is a variegated weave
of wins and losses and altered plans.
Doing the best I can
means sometimes simply making it through the day
using whatever means I'm able to choose.
Even when I lose my self-respect,
making the effort to try again
restores the balance that makes the whole –
always more miracles than mistakes
with grace in place of disgrace.

Wholly Committed To Me

If I don't stop this,
it's going to kill God.

*So we'll go together,
because it's certainly killing you.*

I'm addicted to sin, stubborn self-will,
reticent refusal to quit my misery.
My pet sin is like a pet rock,
unable to slither away on it's own,
and when I throw it out, the thing boomerangs
and I'm back to square one.

*Can I put in my perspective?
You are already wholly committed to me.*

What?

*Few of my children
name their sins with absolute integrity.
You seek me, talk with me constantly
and wrestle with your helplessness.
I long to hear from everyone,
no matter what they say,
and I honor your persistence,
which I reckon to you as faith,
like Abraham and David –
big time sinners, just like you.
But they came back to me over and over,
and I called them friends, as I honor you.
Did you hear that?
As I love you.
Do you get that?*

*You please me every time
you come and have it out with me.
I'm pleased when you seek my help.
Everyone is precious in my sight,
but I am precious to you
in spite of all your faults and failure.
I know your love is true*

and we'll work on your fickle heart.

You are not alone;
all the great saints (as you call them)
aren't any better than you.
You think they don't battle with sin?
Reconsider –
all of you are broken;
you ALL need redemption, help and hope.

Actually, I planned it that way.
I know the conceit of everyone I made
and that doesn't make me unwilling
to mend your life.
I'd rather have you whopper-jawed
than robots who would do what I want
because I push a button and they obey.
That isn't love, but performance,
and I want your love more than anything else.
In that, you're just like me –
made in my image with a heart for home
where you will be perfect again.
And for now, you're wholly committed.
However long you can do it is victory.
When you fail, repent.

I'll need your help with that.

I'll meet you half-way;
just don't give up.
Groveling isn't a virtue.
But you ARE wholly committed, so try again.
A hundred times a day is OK,
and I'll hold your hand
while you practice this plan.
Get it? Got it? Let's go.

Thank you with all my heart.

Fertile Dirt of the Heart

There's a hole in my hand
where they crucified Jesus,
dug with a spade
that severed the roots of beauty beneath my garden,
undermining the green in me.

It's deceptively easy to coast through life
accepting duty in treasonous trade
for passion that pokes holes in me
and works it's way out from within.
I've lost sight of my vision,
but not the scent of fertile dirt
sheltered in my primal heart so full of life
that it creeps into dreams to contact me,
weeps up in longing I've set aside
until I cannot abide this division of life and heart –
the inseparable twins I've forced to function alone.
For I'm afraid to find freedom from fear,
afraid to be found by the predator
that stalks me into endless doing that never is enough
and devours dreams while immature
before they can be born.

Dear God, rise up in me
fiercer than fear, louder than logic.
Let my roots grasp water and earth
that I may create and thrive.

Growth

Growth is over and above,
never finite, finished, frail,
as a tree keeps reaching up and out,
roots keep digging down
to support the ever added leaves,
with rings around the trunk
to record the years of life.
And I sense the up and out in me
as faith sprouts leaves and wings,
even when I'm dormant in my winter,
wilted, wanting, still,
when God says,

Rest and wait;
keep your branches up.
This darkness isn't dead,
for you will leaf again in season
when you're ready to try again.

Even when I feel no hope or help,
no courage, calm, or meaning,
my roots hang onto Mother Earth
who holds me where I am.

I'm not like Jesus –
bursting from the tomb that tied him down.
But God renews my life in teaspoons,
tiny traces of breath inhaled
and little leaves look out
and then explore the unknown outside world.
I take no leaps of faith, but trust in tentative risks –
the only way for me to discover
if the miracle works for me.
And God rewards the simplest touch of faith
with trust to try again.
This is how I gain my growth,
my life for all to see,
and I'm amazed to find me standing tall
from life inside this tree.

Perseverance

Crawling out from under my rock
at four in the morning
has singular rewards.
In the dark before dawn,
my thoughts are clear like starlight.
Emerging emotions lie sorted by sleep
and God has his best chance of reaching me
until pain imposes peace restraints
and my prayers condense
to "Help me, God"
repeated like a rosary.

Why are good drugs always bad for you?
I know my strength came from perseverance
and growth is slow or not at all,
but isn't there merit
in sudden solace sometimes?
Do you understand?

You were perfect, period –
never late, always good
or you wouldn't be God.
I don't understand, but trust you anyway
mixed with doubt,
start every day with "Thy will be done,"
then renege and return to the faith-go-round,
but willing to crawl from under my rock
into your arms tomorrow.

Giving Up Giving Up

I was going to say
I was stressed (which I was),
but that's no excuse.
The cause of my failure is weakness –
one of my strongest character traits.
Pride is no excuse today,
for all I feel is defeated,
discouraged, dis-everything.
I'm glad you love me
because right now I don't.

God, I want so badly
for you to be proud of me,
for *me* to be proud of me.
There's no way this side of heaven to be sin-free,
but I actually had hope this morning
to at least have more victory than normal.
I had no expectation
of the sin attached to me like a tumor
to just fall off,
but I really hoped there would be improvement today,
not my usual loss of self-respect.

Am I ever going to be your "good and faithful servant"
instead of this...slug?
That's what I feel like.
How can I ever tell someone how you transformed me
when it hasn't happened to me yet?
When is the miracle going to happen to me?

It is happening, but perhaps so slowly
you can't see it like I can.
Most of my miracles are slow.
Do flowers explode out of the ground in full bloom?
Jack's beanstalk is fiction;
real beanstalks don't reach the heavens ever
and certainly don't become full-grown overnight.
Growth is a process and it's slooooooow.

I know you don't believe this,
but you already please me

by simply trying to follow my will.
Even becoming willing is a roller coaster ride –
an up and down experience
that may make you want to throw up.

Remember I made
everything and everyone unique
(I don't do leftovers).
All creation lives and dies,
grows and heals at different rates,
in different seasons.
That's a lot more interesting
than the same ol' same 'ol.

Now about your ingrown sin –
of course I hate it, much more than you do,
but I'm proud of you for fighting.
You're a champion of faith in me.
No, don't tune me out – you know I don't lie.
Giving in isn't giving up.
Remember when you used to do both?

One of the transformations I've brought about in your life
is you gave up giving up.
Now you believe in hope.
Today you long for
righteousness and holiness
rather than running off screaming.
You seek me rather than avoid me.
No one admits they've screwed up
to someone they don't trust.
No one keeps on asking me for help
if they don't believe it will do any good.

Your passion for growth isn't a human instinct;
I have to train you for that,
and you're teachable.
I can't teach someone who isn't willing to learn.
A wounded, imperfect Jesus-follower
planted the seed of faith in you
and you proved to be fertile ground (not futile ground).
Someone watered you,
but I gave you Miracle Grow.

Uncensored Prayer

Don't be so hard on yourself.
I granted you grace;
would you please extend some to yourself?
You're never gonna get it all right on the planet,
but you remain
alright by me.

Chapter 13

Pain

Pain flattens you. "Flat as a pancake" is a lie. Pancakes are poufy little discs; the bottom of the skillet is flat. Anyone who has survived a divorce, contracted a debilitating disease, lost a job, or lost their home understands what pain is like. Pain comes in a broad range of degrees, but it all hurts.

The pain I remember forever is devastating. When I'm burning at the stake through my heart, pain is my universe. All other realities are dead, thoughts and language are raw and dark, and the only light is the fire. God alone can reach me, and He speaks through His embrace that I can't feel, but I still cry to Him, knowing He hears. Prayer is reduced to "Oh God oh God," and I sob long after the well is empty, dreading a comfortless dawn.

Only those who have lived in hell understand. Only a Savior who has died from this agony and lived to tell the tale is sufficient to be our God.

He was despised and rejected by mankind,
a man of suffering, and familiar with pain.
Like one from whom people hide their faces
he was despised, and we held him in low esteem.

Surely he took up our pain
and bore our suffering,
yet we considered him punished by God,
stricken by him, and afflicted.
But he was pierced for our transgressions,
  he was crushed for our iniquities;

> *the punishment that brought us peace was on him,*
> *and by his wounds we are healed.* Isaiah 53:3-5 (NIV)

From the cross, Jesus wailed,

> *My God, my God, why hast thou forsaken me?*
> *Far from my deliverance are the words of my groaning.*
> *Oh my God, I cry by day, but thou dost not answer;*
> *and by night, but I have no rest.* Psalm 22:1-2 (NASB)

David understood. He wrote,

> *Save me, O God,*
> *For the waters have threatened my life.*
> *I have sunk in deep mire, and there is no foothold;*
> *I have come into deep waters, and a flood overflows me.*
> *I am weary with my crying; my throat is parched;*
> *My eyes fail while I wait for my God.* Psalm 69:1-3 (NASB)

This is the most personal chapter in the book, the writing that's the most difficult for me to let you read. Yet it may be the most important. I feel if I don't let you see me at my lowest, you might miss how crucial it is for you to be completely honest with God when you're at your worst. God doesn't care what you say; what's important to Him is that you say it, come to Him as you are without editing anything, without worrying if what you say is appropriate or right or sane. He is the ultimate safe place. You can't offend Him, and He will keep your confidences.

God understands pain. He feels it everyday, not just through empathy, but because so much in the world breaks His heart. All the zillions of people who reject Him and curse Him cuts God to the core. Who is He going to talk with about His anguish? Only those who understand and come to Him through Uncensored Prayer, when they are at the bottom of a deep well with their face in the mud. Only someone like you.

Oh, how well I know this unmitigated pain. But even when God is silent, I still seek Him in Uncensored Prayer. There's nowhere else to go, no one else I can tell. Why do I reach out to God when I feel so alone and neglected, sobbing and out of options? I've learned this isn't the end of the story.

> *In You our fathers trusted; They trusted and You delivered them.*
>
> *To You they cried out and were delivered; In You they trusted and were not disappointed.* Psalm 22:4-5 (NASB)

I don't know why God doesn't always ease my anguish when I need it the most, but even then I sense Him caring, loving, hurting that I'm hurting. Perhaps He knows this is the only way for me to gain strength to endure darkness, to trust Him to take care of me even when I can't feel it. In a previous poem, I wrote,

Could it be that He loves me enough to leave me alone,

enduring the pain along with me,

suffers to lay aside sudden salvation

so I can gain strength from bearing my cross,

believing beyond circumstantial deprivation

to see the invisible restoration to come –

resurrection of life that cannot be achieved

without death and delay of Sunday's dawn.

God's mercy and redemption are stronger than any pain, and His love will heal every heart that reaches out to Him. Hold onto God in the dark places. He's got you in his arms and won't ever let you go.

In this chapter, I share the despair that results from unmitigated pain that God doesn't seem to relieve. When partial faith is all we have, it's easy to believe God prefers people who appear to us as "saints", that He's proud of them, not us, because they are devoted to God, following Him without deviation. But even though God loves us equally, those of us who feel certain we can never please God have an opportunity that those sure of their salvation might not experience: reaching out to God when we feel we have no other option allows Him to reach into our deepest dark proving He loves us, no matter what.

Bleed Like Me

Ambushed by tears again,
sobbing my way when most inconvenient
when all I want is solitude to cry in pieces.
Oh to be able to cry when sad
and not whenever my body says.

Do you know what I mean, Jesus?
Did you bleed to death
before they drained you dry on the cross?
In the garden alone, no one heard;
not even the Father was home.
Alone without your small group
of chicken disciples asleep to your panic;
they meant well but melted
when it cost more than they were able to give.
Wanting to be strong wasn't enough,
not yet, but not forever.

See, there's hope for me.
Yeah, you already know
but I forget, yet you don't forget me.
You know, you remember,
you know my pain.
You still bleed along with me.

Partial Faith

Hooray for the victors who win the acclaim,
pay their all and achieve success,
applause and medals, affirmation and praise.
I mean it – they deserve recognition.

But what of those who give their best
and are never renowned except with pity,
fame for shame of failure again,
who earn crumbs for not quitting this time
until perhaps they reach the bottom of the well.
How many times can you miss the mark
without facing this isn't your gift from God?
Why cry and try for what you can't have –
salvation for others, not me?
We're exempt for failure to trust
and let go 100% like them who fit in.

Does God shrug and say,

Let me know when you're ready,
when your will no longer works for you?

What if partial faith is the best we have,
with no trust in people who martyr those with less success?

Do they really think we'll volunteer
for pity, slander, and being ignored?
Where do we go except back out
where at least we can succeed at being professional failures?
We don't see God's promises coming true.
What's the use of longing for what you can't have?
We crave, like addicts, to be winners like them.
And those that do, continue to try – at least, many do –
while some die inside or altogether, alone.

God, you said you made me unique and precious,
but I see defection in your design.
I believe and don't,
try hard and won't let go of you,
for the alternative is my own personal hell.

The Only One Safe To Tell

What do you know about sin?
You never did, or had a baby,
failed your father, failed yourself.
You're perfect –
what do you know about guilt?
You're always right, never fuck up,
never leave me when I'm wrong.

Right now, you're not any comfort.
You can't possibly understand
the way it feels to lose the war of trying
never to do it again.
I want to shake you silly, scream in your face.
I want you so bad to know what it's like
to never or always or not enough.

I can't bear this shit right now.
I know you're the great and holy God
and I'm probably sinning to feel this way,
but I can't say these things to anyone else,
how I feel about you and me.
They don't understand;
I don't understand myself.
I sure as hell don't understand you,
but I feel it's safe to tell you,
though I haven't a clue what to do from here.

Help – I hurt so bad, I'm so angry
and don't know why I'm here.
I just want this pain to go away.
I just want to go away
and leave myself behind
where I can't feel, can't see,
can't know anything but peace with myself,
love as I am,
hope that this hell hasn't come to stay,
that this shame and blame aren't all my fault.

I don't know what else to do but tell you.
I don't even care if this prayer is inappropriate.
If it isn't, oh well, what the hell.

What would Jesus do?
Talk to you, tell you, yell at you,
cry to die at you,
refuse to lie to you no matter what.
Well, this is what matters –
it's you or not or nothing.
I don't know where else to go.
Oh God
oh God
oh God.

I don't want to die –
I want to be different.
I want to matter.
Does this matter to you?
I know it does – help me, God.
I can't help myself except to tell you.

Tried, Fried, and Died

No matter what I do, I can't make it work,
can't figure it out like my closest friends who get it.
It's like 3rd grade homework –
I've tried, fried and died
and just threw it against the wall today.
Fuck it;
fuck all y'all.

The last thing I'm going to do
is tell of my hell to the people who matter most
except you.
You're the only one who won't tell anybody.
You pass up pat kindly "there there's,"
or the worst – "let me show you how,"
because what if I still don't understand
this common human achievement?

I know what I'd do –
lie and pretend to cover incompetence.
They get it; why can't I?
I accept you made us each unique,
but this failure isn't sin.
I hate being stupid in ordinary things,
and if you made me like this, I'm mad at you.
You reign from a position of complete control,
so this says something about you.

Did you have a bad day when you created me?
Did you need a cosmic joke,
a token misfit in the universe to balance the better souls?
I can't reconcile this,
and feel abandoned by the only one safe to tell,
so I'm medicating under my rock.
You want me?
You know where I am.

I don't give a shit about perseverance,
Christian courage et. al.
I'll protect myself from everyone else
until I can lie convincingly
or find the guts to be myself, regardless of reputation.

That risk is what Jesus took, didn't he?
But he was God and could take it,
make it into the gospel statement
left in poor hands to save the world.

Is that what I am –
poor hands to save myself or others?
Been there, am that with a Master's degree.
I know pain, not your plan
and am not sure I can commit to your call
whenever it comes.

All I know for sure
is I'm lost and you're found.
My belief in you is steady,
but my trust in my well-being ebbs and flows.
Yeah, I know what the Bible says,
but I also know how I feel and fail.

I have no faithful following
or regular righteousness.
You say all my righteousness
comes from you, and I believe that,
but aren't true believers mostly consistent
in trying to live like you?
You and I follow each other,
impartial partners, though you're the reliable one.
I feel like when I get to heaven,
the crown awaiting me will come from Burger King,
painted paper compared to real jewels.

Do I embarrass you?
Do you hang with me because you know
I'll be a jackass on my own?
Is that true for everyone?
So why do I feel so isolated
from the rest of the redeemed?

I know I'm scared shitless
from the earthly versions of Billy Graham,
Mother Teresa martyrs
giving their lives to serve others
as a way of serving you.

Uncensored Prayer

I really admire them, though I'm a hundred lives away.

I know you're proud of them,
those "good and faithful servants."
They make me want to throw up and scream and cry
because I'm not like that,
and I'm afraid to ask you
if they're honor students who get scholarships
in All Saints Academy
while I crouch in the bushes,
jealous and disdainful, judgmental out of fear,
not that they'd judge me,
but that you're disappointed in me.
I'm a dishwasher in the party upstairs,
a liver in the Body of Christ with cirrhosis
with equal parts of doubt and faith.

Do you still want me like this?
Do you?
I'm afraid to ask.
I know you love me,
but I desperately want you
to like me like them.

Unhealed Heart

Rip –
the tears tear down my face
leaked from veins just underneath the skin
from the heart pump in my dark.

*My tears bled down my face, too,
for you –
drained from my heart
big enough for sin in all the world,
all the you's who need me.*

Like me?

*Like you. And I love you, tears and all,
ripped and ragged unhealed heart.*

Great theology lesson –
now will you leave me alone?

*Sorry – no can do.
I can't bear to die without you,
leave you alone and lost.
You cost a lot, child.*

So save someone worth saving.

There isn't anyone worse or better than you.

I'm not sure…
what do you gain from this deal?

*Someone to love,
maybe someone to love me.
Isn't that what you want, too?*

Yeah, well…I guess "yes."

Can we hang out together?

Kinda like dating?

That'll do.
You know I love you.

Me, too – really.
I just hurt today.

I understand...
sometimes I hurt, too.

Chapter 14

Grace

Grace is God's unmerited favor and love for us. But it's not always easy to deal with. Grace often feels like allowing someone to get away with something. We like it when God gives it to us, but we're not always comfortable giving it to others.

> *For it is by grace you have been saved, through faith—and this is not from yourselves, it is the gift of God—not by works, so that no one can boast. Ephesians 2:8-9 (NIV).*

An excellent example of this is the parable Jesus told known as The Prodigal Son. One of two sons asked his father for his inheritance, which the father gave him. The young man squandered all of it in decadent living, until he was broke and had nowhere to go. He knew he had messed up really bad, and thought about going home and asking his dad for forgiveness.

> *So he got up and went to his father.*

> *But while he was still a long way off, his father saw him and was filled with compassion for him; he ran to his son, threw his arms around him and kissed him. Luke 15:20 (NIV)*

> *But the father said to his servants, "Quick! Bring the best robe and put it on him. Put a ring on his finger and sandals on his feet. Bring the fattened calf and kill it. Let's have a feast and celebrate. For this son of mine was dead and is alive again; he was lost and is found." So they began to*

celebrate. Luke 15:22-24 (NIV)

When the son who had stayed home, working hard, heard about the party going on for his spendthrift brother, he got really mad at his dad and chewed him out. I'm certain the father's answer made no sense to his son nor changed his mind, because dad was showing grace and forgiveness.

"My son," the father said, "you are always with me, and everything I have is yours. But we had to celebrate and be glad, because this brother of yours was dead and is alive again; he was lost and is found." Luke 15:31-32 (NIV)

Thankfully, God has no favorites, because we're all guilty of screwing up.

For we all often stumble and fall and offend in many things. James 3:2 (AMP)

Unlike our justice system, God has no lists of big sins and little sins. Stealing a paper clip is the same as chainsaw murder to Him.

For whoever keeps the whole law and yet stumbles at just one point is guilty of breaking all of it. For he who said, "You shall not commit adultery," also said, "You shall not murder." If you do not commit adultery but do commit murder, you have become a lawbreaker. James 2:10-11 (NIV)

Grace isn't license to do whatever we want, and then just saying, "Sorry" to make it all better. But God's grace does mean He is willing to forgive us, no matter what we've done or will do. It's not about us. It's what God has chosen to do, because He can, because His love for us supersedes every one of our faults and mistakes. That's kind of scary, if you think about it.

Why would He do that? And what if he changes His mind?

Can you ask God questions like that? Sure. That's what Uncensored Prayer is all about. God thinks there's no risk at all in talking with Him about whatever. We're the ones who are afraid God has a hidden booby-trap, and if we say the wrong thing talking with Him, we're toast. It's easy to wonder if offending God is the unforgiveable sin.

I've come to believe that God can't be offended by anything we think or say. I'm proof of that. If God can be offended, I would have done it and this would be a very different book called, *Censored Prayer: What Not to Say to God.*

But it's not. This is a book about opening up to a sense of freedom that comes from grace. I still wonder and worry about it sometimes, usually when my brain is in panic mode and I've weirded out. Here's a fear-busting word from God:

> *Therefore let us draw near with confidence to the throne of grace, so that we may receive mercy and find grace to help in time of need. Hebrews 4:16 (NASB)*

Don't be afraid of God. He's not out to get you or trap you. He is out to surprise you with how wonderful He really is. You have to spend time with Him to find that out yourself. God has a bad reputation about judgment, anger, and retribution. Let Him set the record straight. Go ahead – talk with Him.

This section addresses the fact that God's grace is irrelevant to those who think they don't need it. Denial that we wish there was more to life than our very best can achieve prevents us from experiencing the wholeness only God can provide. Facing our inability to satisfy the hunger in our hearts allows God to meet our deepest desires and more than we can imagine possible: peace, unfailing love, and hope when all else fails.

Your Name Is "Yet"

Redemption always starts with you,
the least likely to ransom the Murder Book
that only lists my name.
My fame for successful addictions
to other gods gives me comfort
because I can do it.
I'm good at hurting you and me
and others who really care
but offer sadness, sympathy or silent blame.
They know it's my choice to stay the same.
What I don't hear is understanding
of my battle to win and lose.
I want both, so stay in my chosen cage
'cause I'm tired of failing to win.
It embarrasses me.

You understand;
you won't reinforce my shame
and never set conditions for acceptance.
You know, I'd feel a whole lot better
if you'd judge and then just leave me to rot,
like the people who've said, "Come see me
when you've decided to get off
the see-saw and trust in saving grace."
I can't face that yet, so sit stranded in pain
because I'm afraid surrender will hurt more
than I can dare.

You make me crazy 'cause you won't abandon me
to hang out only with faithful believers
comforted by grace.
I've got much more faith than a mustard seed,
but my mountain stays in place,
which can only mean my pumpkin seed won't work.

I feel so alone, so frightened to try and trust you
because I can't with all my heart.
They say I haven't hit bottom yet,
but my bottom is adios from here
to take my chances on the other side.

Yet you have a great track record of saving my ass
all the times I've tried to die
by taking reckless risks and surviving the odds
that aren't possible but for you,
which can only mean
that you won't leave when I'm willing to leave myself,
when everyone I love
is "concerned for me" or given up.

So many people say "God is love" or "good"
or "Savior" or "Lord."
You know what first occurs to me when I think of you?
Your name is "Yet" no matter what –
yet you love me and stay,
yet you want me, period,
yet you believe in me when I can't believe in you.

So why is it so hard to trust you, God,
with all I am and have?
Why am I terrified to take your hand then jump,
arms locked around your neck,
my legs wrapped 'round your waist,
and stop worrying about my inability
to have courage or strength of character?
If I'm in your arms, it's your responsibility to carry me
until I heal enough to walk on my own.

Make it possible for me to touch the "Yet" you are.
I keep coming and stop, yet you run the remaining 99%.
You're willing to leap the chasm I can't cross
and be the "Yet" I need.
"Thank you, I love you" is all I can honestly say,
and yet it's enough for you.

To the dread I face, to the hesitation,
to the total belief "I can't,"
I name this now to you
and come all I can
and know that I'll come again.

God's Justice

One time can make a baby;
one act can result in prison for life.
There are no guarantees you won't be caught
or betrayed by family and friends.
One stupid choice in a single moment
or as many waves in the sea
roll over and over us,
patterns of habits learned
and addiction to destruction.

No one is exempt.
The person that feels
protected by prayer and clean living
is just as susceptible to sudden sin,
like pushing someone in passion a little too hard –
the concussion killed.
"I didn't mean to" doesn't cut it with the judge
about unintentional neglect
of the baby forgotten in an overheated car.

In God's justice, there are no little sins
that are better than felony failures.
We're all criminals breaking God's holiness,
unfixable on our own.
Only God in flesh could pay a price
big enough to redeem us from slavery.

Thank you, Jesus, for loving us enough
to give your best for us, to us
and one with us.
Set us free forever from fear of God
next time we fail.

Unmerited Favor

Jesus saves me –
a full-time job,
more angels than usual to protect my sorry ass.
The thought comes to me often
how disastrous my life would have been without him,
probably over long ago
considering how many train wrecks I've survived.

Odds didn't exist –
only God's grace: "unmerited favor"
that makes no sense to me.
Why would he help our sorry selves?
I really worry about God's sanity sometimes.
I mean, who watches out for him?

All creation is well-designed but us.
Jesus lived and died to redeem every rock and tree,
four-legged, two-legged, no-legged life and water and sand,
the whole enchilada.
Yet saving people is the most bizarre;
maybe he knows we need the most help.
That's a fact that factors in every action off the mark,
all thoughts and wants and could-have-beens.

I'm a could-have-been for sure,
yet he made me as I am,
wanting my choice of love more than obedience
or even humble surrender.
For me, at least, neither follows
my desperate craving for love
which he gives, no matter how I respond.
I just don't get it and can't give it, either,
neither does he renege.

Oh God, my best is hilarious,
but I can't let go of seeking you for you –
the one I want the most to want me
whether I'm faithful or not.

A Wounded Child

Misery loves God,
when it's so much easier to pray.
When I can't slay my own dragons,
I call for royal assistance and he does his thing,
not to my credit at all,
because he's like that –
loving me when I'm not likeable,
when I'm only a whiny jerk and merit his inattention
and still he calls me his friend.

Can you beat that?
He's a dad who should make me
go to my room on a time out
until I can talk reasonably.
But I'm not reasonable when I'm hurting –
that's when I'm self-centered,
thinking only about my pain.
He should be ashamed of me – I would be.

Why does he come running,
giving his best when I'm less than candid
about my part in our relationship?
When I'm dying inside, me is all I see;
thinking is eclipsed by deep heart hurt.
And that's when God is divine,
with no division in his love,
no collision between grace and law,
enabling me, finally,
to relax in his arms –
a wounded child protected in the dark.

Chapter 15

Addiction

I am addicted to several things, and know well the pain, conflict, and vice-grip hold. I have no defense against this. Nada. Zilch. Many friends with similar addictions have been immensely helpful and supportive, as I've battled with this disease. But God alone has the power to deliver me. Giving control to God over my life and addictions is *the* most important thing I do every day.

In an ironic sense, this is an advantage that recovering addicts have over non-addicts. We know the seriousness of surrendering to God. We do it or die. That may seem overly dramatic, but it's a fact for addicts. Without God's intervention, our disease may literally kill us.

Solomon seems to have been an addict, too. What he wrote says it all.

> *Who has woe? Who has sorrow? Who has strife? Who has complaining? Who has wounds without cause? Who has redness and dimness of eyes?*

> *Those who tarry long at the wine, those who go to seek and try mixed wine.*

> *Do not look at wine when it is red, when it sparkles in the wineglass, when it goes down smoothly.*

> *At the last it bites like a serpent and stings like an adder.*

> *[Under the influence of wine] your eyes will behold strange things [and loose women] and your mind will utter things

> turned the wrong way [untrue, incorrect, and petulant].
>
> Yes, you will be [as unsteady] as he who lies down in the midst of the sea, and [as open to disaster] as he who lies upon the top of a mast.
>
> You will say, They struck me, but I was not hurt! They beat me [as with a hammer], but I did not feel it! When shall I awake? I will crave and seek more wine again [and escape reality].
>
> Proverbs 23:29-35 (AMP)

Non-addicts might not suffer such dire consequences if they don't allow God to be Lord of their lives, but victory over their own faults and weaknesses will be equally limited. The solution for all of us is the same.

> For the LORD your God is the one who goes with you to fight for you against your enemies to give you victory.
> Deuteronomy 20:4 (NIV)

This one sentence is loaded with hope for all of us. We don't fight our battles with sin alone; God is with us. God fights *for* us to give us victory if He is our Lord. 'Nuf said.

Here's another gem:

> Do not fear **them**, for the LORD your **God is the one fighting for you.** Deuteronomy 3:22 (NASB)

"Them" is fill-in-the-blank for us personally: people, sin, addictions, shame, whatever applies. God promises to **fight for us** about all of that. For it to benefit us, we have to cooperate with Him. We have to partner with God for our own good, not just lie down on the train track hoping the train won't run over us because God will stop the train.

My husband, Bud, also partners with me for our good. We're both addicts. He's never had a slip, while I've been out and in several times. Every time I've gone back out, even for long periods of time, Bud has never altered his unconditional love for me, and never nagged. I don't know if I could keep my mouth shut like that if our situations were reversed.

Just like God, Bud has proven his commitment to me with his grace and forgiveness, which gives me the support I need to choose recovery again when I'm ready. To give up something I love that is destructive requires enough love for myself and God to gain health and freedom. Paul wrote:

> *I once thought these things were valuable, but now I consider them worthless because of what Christ has done. Yes, everything else is worthless when compared with the infinite value of knowing Christ Jesus my Lord. For his sake I have discarded everything else, counting it all as garbage, so that I could gain Christ and become one with him. I no longer count on my own righteousness through obeying the law; rather, I become righteous through faith in Christ. For God's way of making us right with himself depends on faith. Philippians 3:7-9 (NLT)*

Paul makes a true point that recovery involves surrender. For all of us, following God means God is in front and we're not (duh). It means He's in charge, and our job is to follow directions, even though we're inconsistent about that.

This is extremely hard for me, even though I know my way doesn't work, and God scores a perfect 10 every time. God will allow us to compromise and cut corners all we want, but if we spend time with Him, He'll be the one to initiate wrestling with us. That's how badly He wants us to get the deep soul satisfaction, which only He can give.

Do you want freedom from anything that holds you back, chains you to a wall?

Are you willing to struggle with God? Maybe?

You're thinking about it, aren't you. Even if you've practiced Uncensored Prayer for a long time, you're thinking about the thing you won't let go, and the thing you've been wrestling about with God to which you still say "Maybe" or "Later".

Good.

In this chapter I reveal my on again/off again battle with addiction. God loves and accepts us no matter what, even if we're never able or willing to change negative behavior. We all have habits or sins that re-occur with frustrating regularity. The Bible says none of us will be perfect on earth. Weaknesses and failures are a part of being human. The good news is God forgives everything. He made us like we are, knowing that only failure will bring us back to Him, because God has granted us free-will, so that loving Him and seeking redemption are voluntary. God gives us a zillion chances, not to get things right, but to start again fresh every time.

My Chosen Cross

Split like a tree from a single base
that grows two trunks with parallel lives,
I divided in childhood into fraternal twins –
yin yang identities that linger still.
And I crave them both to my chagrin,
shedding sin like skin in spiritual growth
while clinging to familiar favorites
that I want to release but can't,
in spite of my will to be whole,
wholly trusting my God
who waits and wants it more than me.
God help me release these ingrown nails
that connect me to my chosen cross.
Help me where I can't help myself
and haul me out of this hole.

Want To/Don't Want To

Why can't I lay this down?
Why won't I?
This addiction to the past,
the obsession to retain the hurt that haunts me,
causes me to perpetuate self-condemning action
that mutates from vice to foe,
that keeps me chained to all I hate
and claim I long to leave.
And yet I practice like a pro
receiving praise from no one,
no reward, no promise of relief
while I hang on and hang myself
with what I hate to lose.

You have promised power to free me,
all the help I need to heal.
What's wrong with me?
Am I proud or stupid to choose death over life?
I fight deliverance like it's the bad guy
who stalks to take me down.
I'm miserable, embarrassed, angry at myself
and yet here I am – a life-long fool
enmeshed in a mess of my making.

Why don't you do something, God?
Zap me like Paul;
take me away where I can't hurt myself.
Intervene in my destruction,
haul me off to heaven – the land of the free –
where I will sin no more.

What if I never grow beyond this trap,
my self-imposed exile from grace?
What if I'm never able to trust you enough?
I want to but can't;
every attempt is short-lived,
fraught with frustration as I cry to you,
"I'm sorry" once again.

What kind of child am I to act this way,
repenting without belief that it will matter in an hour

when I know I'll fail again, and yet I keep trying.
Does that make sense?
You stand with open arms;
in fact, you hold me close and whisper love
that somehow isn't enough.

I see these Christians
who tell amazing tales of salvation at the brink.
I long for this so bad it hurts like hell
because it doesn't happen for me.
I know I hope or I wouldn't seek it,
wouldn't try to grasp this grace.

You say I can't do it, but you can;
my best will never save my soul.
You say you came because I couldn't come.
You follow me around
like a stray puppy I cannot shake;
you sit within my pain and it hurts you, too.
I see your eyes – compassionate and kind –
but what about those who want to trust, but can't,
who long for love, but lose?

Can you help someone who can't do their part
to believe and just let go?
Am I stuck with half a heart
to serve you with the whole of me?
Where's the hope for me –
divided and doubting deliverance once for all?

God don't leave me like this;
don't let go of me.
You put up with Peter and Thomas –
prime examples of un-likely disciples.
You say you won't abandon me,
but please God don't abandon me.
I'm the least likely to succeed at this;
please don't give up on me.

The Dilemma

Oh my God.

You're right.

I don't really trust you
to free me from my addictions.

You're wrong.

Well…I don't really trust me to let you.

You're right. It takes both of us or it won't work.
Your cooperation is essential for me to help you.

Well, here's the problem:
I want to and don't want to at the same time.

Name it.

There's nothing that feels as good as using
and nothing that feels as bad
as the guilt and shame of not beating this thing.
I'm having trouble of letting go of the feel-good feelings
and the guilt/shame part can't compete.

What if I told you that surrendering your drugs of choice
could make you feel better than your highest high?

I've been told that by true believers,
but I'm afraid of the unavoidable pain and grief of loss.

That's valid and true.
Loss of any love hurts like hell
and takes a long time to heal,
but I promise to stay extra close to you through it.

Where's the epidural through the pain of this birth?

There isn't one.

And you want me to volunteer for this?

*There's no alternative to get through it,
past it to a place where you'll feel really good about yourself.
Are you ready for a shock?
You'll feel really good, too.
It's like you love chocolate because of M&Ms,
but I'm telling you that rich, deeply satisfying dark chocolate
is your for the taking,
but first you have to dump the M&Ms.*

How do I know this will happen for me?

You don't, but have I ever lied to you?

Not that I'm aware of.

What makes you think I picked today to start?

The issue here is my ability to trust either of us.
So how am I supposed to handle this?
I'm stuck like a butterfly on a mat unable to fly.

If I pull the pin, you'll soar.

You know my dilemma:
I'm afraid to let go of what I know for sure.

*That makes sense. But what if?
Are you willing to consider that?
All you have to risk is release won't work for you.
There are exceptions to everything.
Some people don't get the deal;
it doesn't happen for them.*

So you can't guarantee success?

Nope.

So why try?

*What if it works?
How will you know until you try?
If it doesn't, I'll give you a full refund.*

*You can keep the best you know
and regain your dilemma.*

And?

And?

I don't know if I can do this.

*That's understandable.
It's your choice to move forward or not.
Either way I love you as you are.
Want to see what we can do together?
Are you willing to try?*

Yes.

It's a deal.

Surrendering is a Bitch

So I hear you're ready.

Yes, but...

Surrendering is a bitch, isn't it?

Oh yes, and fear is working overtime,
not of you, but me.

*That's a given.
Everyone's like that.*

You've got to be kidding.

*Even the best-looking saints are scared
that they can't keep up their end of the deal,
and sometimes they don't.
But in surrendering to me,
commitment doesn't mean perfection
and I certainly don't require it.
Giving over everything
means risking your best with all you are
and trusting me if you slip.*

So if I screw this thing up, it's your fault?

*Very funny – ha, ha.
But it isn't your fault, either.
You're flawed, but not fatally.
You've made a huge decision to surrender,
and I honor this, and will help you all you'll let me,
even in spite of you as needed.*

*But you're a complete novice
at turning you vices and visions over to me.
Surrendering is a learning process—
like learning to play the piano.
You're going to suck at first,
but don't give up on either of us.
People who lay down their addictions
and have a time and date in their pocket*

*have no claim on will-power,
and no promise of falling again, ever,
until moving into my house.
Success is an act of faith, not arrival.*

You're asking an awful lot for me to believe this.

*Having faith isn't based on having belief, though it helps.
Many times faith is so intangible
you'll feel it's gone.
But acting on faith,
whether you believe it will work or not,
is an extraordinary step of courage.
Just trust me tomorrow between sleeping and sleeping,
and I'll help you have faith in yourself,
in spite of your self- doubts,
your self-everythings.
OK?*

OK.

OK.

The Tangled Wad of Yarn

He said it was time –
he and his vice of forty years
were estranged and getting a divorce.
I'm shocked. I thought they would never part.
You're in the miracle business,
but WOW,
and yet I know you intervened for me
and my precious vice is gone.

Vice #2 trembles at the thought,
but I'm not ready to drop it down.
I dread the coming separation –
permanently, I hope.
Just don't do it too soon, OK?

I know, I know....
I'm not conceding to co-operate,
to let go and let you take it.
Funny, how I'm not beating myself up.
You had a major role in that,
because you're not beating me up.
Your patience astounds me;
at least I'm not afraid of you.

"The fullness of time" isn't here yet
and when it comes, I know you'll help me help myself.
The fiction of my control over life still deceives me.
I can be so damn dumb when I want to,
making dragons up to fight,
insistently resistant to your promised perfect peace.
I'm a pain in the ass, even to myself.

Oh God, my life is such a tangled wad of yarn…
here – see what you can do with it.

Contentment Beats Control

I'm a turtle half out of my shell
about this commitment thing,
and I've figured out what's wrong.
With your help, I successfully surrendered
my worst addiction to you with wonderful results.
I'm free, and have no desire to go back.
Major miracle here.

But my other addiction...
I'm not ready to let it go
and you won't take my responsibility.
"One at a time," I said,
and I think that was a good decision.
But now it's time to give up the other,
and the addiction and I are hanging onto each other
for dear hell.

I guess I'm being a controlling, selfish brat.
Am I proud of this? Yes and no.
I guess that's progress,
but honesty here doesn't resolve my dilemma.
I have to become willing and humble.
There is no going forward from here
without uncompromised obedience to you.

My definition of obedience
is doing something I don't want to do,
well-learned in childhood.
It's right up there with cleaning up
dog poop land mines in the backyard.
So you gave me a different word: contentment,
inserted on a printed page,
plugged into an audio book
where you knew I'd find it
several times in the last twenty-four.

You interfere a lot to save my ass.
I knew it was you
when the word burst out from all the rest.
Sometimes your small, still voice
has to scream for me to listen.

"Surrender" morphed into "contentment"
without my knowing when or how
that first time several weeks ago.
I know the craving will come back someday
but I am no longer afraid of it.
I know what to do, and believe I will.
And now I know what to do
with this other unruly pest –
my heart.

Not today, but soon
I will crave contentment more than control
and fall into your arms –
free from serving stubborn tyrants,
especially myself.

Just Like That

Why am I always surprised
when you keep your promises?
Maybe because I feel like the 13th disciple –
the one who didn't make the cut.
You know how hard it was
when I finally surrendered to you.
Obey is such a negative word.
First, you removed my nemesis – just like that –
then you filled two gaping holes up to the rim,
brimming with your sufficiency.
Why me?

I'm not like Mary, hymen intact,
asked to bear your son and she said, "OK" – just like that –
without thinking what her parents and Joseph would say.
When the angel left, did she suddenly wail,
"Oh my God, have I lost my mind?
What kind of idiot am I?"
Nah…she had hyper faith that I don't share.
Maybe she didn't care about the consequences,
knowing you would take care of her,
which brings me back to my present shock
that you would solve things for me.

What do you see in this she of little faith,
a tugboat in the Atlantic
dodging icebergs and sea monsters twice my size?
You sauntered across the ocean
holding a life vest tailor-made, and said,

Jump on out. The water sucks, but I'm trained in CPR.

What kind of idiot was I to acquiesce to your ridiculous command?
Someone all out of other options;
you're my "when all else fails" God.
Now you're first in my life for the first time ever
and I don't expect that to last,
but I do believe I'll keep bouncing home
on the yo-yo string in your hand.

Chapter 16

Friends

We need friends; God planned it that way.

When I was young, one of the first Bible verses I learned in Sunday School was a simple and short verse. It said:

A friend loveth at all times. Proverbs 17:17 (KJV)

I knew this wasn't true, but I memorized it anyway. Nobody loved all the time, I thought. I didn't understand or experience it until I was an adult.

When I was in the first trimester of pregnancy with my third child, I started bleeding and was rushed to the hospital. Turns out the top third of the placenta had let go, and the doctor told me to stay in bed for the next six months. I already had two pre-schoolers and worked from home. There was no way I could follow the doctor's instructions.

My daddy was a friend of a country doctor, and they discussed my situation. The doctor called me and said, "Repeat after me, 'You got the baby 'till you don't got the baby." I recited the phrase, wondering what it really meant.

The doctor then told me what he meant. He said there was a decent chance I would lose the baby even if I stayed in bed and took care of myself, and a 100% chance I would lose the baby if I didn't. He then repeated himself saying, "Here's what I advise you to do. You got the baby 'till you don't got the baby. You may never hold this child alive in your arms, so name her/him right now and talk to them. Your time together may be very brief, so make the most of it. And *stay in bed*."

I knew the bed part was impossible, but God didn't. People showed up with dinner, ran errands and shopped for me, took the children to a park for the afternoon, cleaned house without my permission. For six months. I didn't have to ask a soul for anything. Word got around, and my friends took over; there were people helping I didn't even know.

In my favorite Bible story, Jesus was teaching in someone's home, and so many people had come to hear him, the crowd extended out the door. Four friends of a paralytic brought him on a pallet to see Jesus, and couldn't get in because of the crowd. So they came up with an ingenious idea. They took their buddy up on the roof, dug a hole (pissing off the homeowner, I'm sure), and lowered their friend down in front of Jesus. Here's the best part of the story:

> *And Jesus seeing **their faith** said to the paralytic, "Son, your sins are forgiven. I say to you, get up, pick up your pallet and go home." Mark 2:5, 11 (NASB)*

Whose faith? *The faith of the friends.* The paralyzed man may not have believed at all. Many times I have lost my faith in God and myself, sunk in black despair that immobilized me. Faithful friends believed on my behalf, and God healed my lack of faith. It's a blessing for me now to do that for others.

The Bible is full of instances where someone introduced a friend or family member to Jesus. John 2:40-48 has two examples. Andrew took his brother, Simon Peter, to Jesus. Phillip brought his friend, Nathanael. John 4 records a conversation Jesus had with a Samaritan woman by a well outside of town.

> *Then, leaving her water jar, the woman went back to the town and said to the people, "Come, see a man who told me everything I ever did. Could this be the Messiah?" They came out of the town and made their way toward him. John 4:28-30 (NIV)*

A friend once gave me a good analogy on this topic. When we fall in love with someone, we can't stop talking about them. So why are we so hesitant to share about Jesus? Why don't we follow his actions? Could it be because he isn't our best friend?

What are my true friends like? They put up with me when I'm a pain in the butt. They love me when I don't love myself. They pray for me when I don't believe. They offer sage advice when I'm nuts, bring dinner in times of trouble, and never abandon me.

I don't believe they treat me with such kindness just to get points with God. I've seen them at their worst, and have bailed them out many times. Jesus treats us like this, which has so deeply impacted our lives that it spills out on others.

Many of us have turned to a close friend when we need compassion or don't know what to do about something. Sometimes in these situations, I just want that person to listen and care. I might feel like I'm in a maze and can't find my way out, or in a cul-de-sac with the exit blocked.

Often my friend has a point of view I hadn't considered, or sees an option I haven't seen. Invariably, if I talk for any length of time, I find myself saying something I didn't realize I knew. A solution or insight has been inside me all along, and I was unaware of it. Strange how that can happen.

The same thing occurs many times when God and I talk. I learn more about myself, not only from God, but from *me*. There's more truth and wisdom inside me than I know. It's easy for me to mistrust what I think, because I've had a lot of great ideas turn out to be great disasters. God helps unravel my tangled perceptions, and He does that many times through my friends.

Nurture the friendships in your life. You need each other now, and when the day comes that one of you needs help in a big way, God won't have to beat the bushes.

This section is about the importance of friends in our lives. We all need people who love us as we are, and are there for us, no matter what. In a unique way, they are God with skin on – His representatives of compassion to whom we relate when we can't see truth for ourselves. True friends understand and offer empathy, not because they have necessarily been through the same situations we have, but because doubt, discouragement, and pain are universal, and they need the same understanding themselves. Such a partnership of love and trust can help us weather storms that might take us down if we felt alone.

Hope In A Basket For A Basket-Case

Most of my life
I've straddled the boundary
between want to/don't want to –
an old friend, an older foe.
Yesterday you sent a friend who held my hand,
and I gained the balance to fall out of the black
a little more toward "Want to,"
something I couldn't do by myself.
But the friend brought hope in a basket and left it,
promising to come again.

A herd of Job's friends have pelted me with judgment,
solutions that worked for them
and therefore would work for me.
When the patient didn't improve,
they removed life support,
declaring it was my fault I hadn't healed.

I've wandered through the wildness,
reticent to reach out again,
having learned that salvation
doesn't come in one-size-fits-all.
A God who makes each snowflake unique,
not destined for replication,
wouldn't devise a universal solution
for each of his hand-made creations.

I believe Jesus is the sole redeemer,
but appears to each of us personalized,
just as a mother's milk is ideal nourishment only for her child.
Other milk is second best at best
and I've tried to try them all,
afraid to rest on the breast of my Mother God,
content, at peace, at home.

My friend reminded me
that prescriptions with proven results
aren't effective for everyone,
might cause harmful reactions, even death.
But I'd never read the fine print,
focused on another failure rather than relief

that I'd been saved from additional injury.
Just because I don't know the cure for me
doesn't mean it isn't there.

I can't alter God's timetable for me
and I'm sure that's a good idea,
but I keep trying manipulation,
protected by my personal Christ.
It baffles me to think you made me this way
(now *there's* a bad idea in my very best futile wisdom).

Yesterday was a candle I haven't blow out.
But today I've been given faith
to believe healing will happen for me
in spite of myself and with my cooperation,
even though I'm not ready now, not yet,
but sometime before I go home with God.
And there's someone with me in addition to you,
sent as a missionary, not to save
 – a deed you've already done –
but as a seeing-eye dog for one behind blinds.

Coffee Pot Friends

OK God, forget everything I said
about happiness, peace, etc.
Today I'm overwhelmed, under secure,
and other feelings without names.
What are you doing to me?

Do I detect panic?

Am I getting through to you?
I've just recovered from surrendering my life to you,
and now this.
How many leaps of faith
do you think I have in me?

It isn't about your faith, child.
I have infinite faith in my plans for you.

Well, I don't.
It took all the trust I had
to risk setting aside what I know about me
to try what I don't know.
Don't you understand that?

Sure I do.
I've asked the impossible of you
and gave you courage to see what I can do.

This is way more than I bargained for.

I promised everything would be OK,
and better than you dreamed.
Has any of this happened yet?

Yeah. I felt more peace and contentment
last week than I've ever had before.
But feelings can lie.

Do I lie?

Not that I've been told.

*Have I told you my plans for your life are wonderful
and that your faith in me will be worth it?
I wasn't kidding.*

Didn't say you were.
But why are you asking me for the world
when I thought you meant the suburbs,
which is already out of my comfort zone.

*Nothing you do with me
will be comfortable or feel safe.
But I've got your back and front
and all around.
I won't let you down
and I won't lead you into danger.*

Easy for you to say –
you do this all the time with other insane people.
But this is new for me,
and if you had anything to do with these people
whose vision for my vision is way out to line…
I don't know what to think.

What makes you think they may be right?

Well, it sounds like you –
plans bigger than I can absorb,
way too much and too fast.
Why would you tell them something
you haven't told me?

*I talk through other people a lot,
and through music, movies, books, nature.
I can talk to you through the coffee pot if I want.*

Are you playing games with me?
I feel stuck on top of a Ferris Wheel
with nobody below to bring me down.

*No, I'm not playing with your vulnerability,
and yes, you're higher up and out
than ever before.
But remember I'm with you*

and will not let you fall or fail.

Fail at following your plan?
I'm trained to screw it up.

*Of course that's your choice
and your history,
but I doubt you'll turn back now.
I gave you serenity last week
because your commitment made it possible
for me to bless you in new ways,
like the mustard seed faith
that moves mountains.
Each time you walk through a door I open,
the new things you'll find
will both scare and delight you.*

Every time?

*I'm afraid so.
Acting in faith towards me is unsettling
because you don't know what will happen.
But it will get easier as you go,
because whenever you follow me,
you'll experience my infallible consistency
in taking care of you.
How's that sound?*

Theoretical but possible.
We already have a track record together,
but mostly off the charts.

*That's normal for me.
I don't do charts, anyway.
I create new paths as I go
with each individual.
Creating is my passion –
new life, new hope,
redemptive freedom for you to "new" yourself.*

My brain has just shorted out.
Can we talk more later?

You bet. Anytime.

Friends With Flashlights

Religion fucked me up,
sucked me into no-win land
where God doesn't live.
It wasn't my fault I was raised that way –
a belief system true for my parents,
and I honor that for them,
but religion didn't honor me.
It took me hostage to rules and reg's
I thought were required by God
to enter into the Holy Land
one scary unknown day.
In the mean time, I was the unredeemed,
un-chosen for what I did,
but mainly for who I was –
the un-elect who couldn't do the deal.

How did that make me feel?
A loser lost to ever pleasing God –
someone I wanted to love me,
but he wouldn't hear my prayers
due to my regarded, heartful sins.
So I was screwed,
condemned to futile attempts
to get saved just right,
say the magic prayer on faith I didn't feel.
I was co-dependent as hell,
trying to please an unpleasable God
who shrugged his shoulders and said,

I'm sorry, but goats don't go to heaven.

Hell came before heaven

'cause you had to die to enter eternal bliss,
but my heart already lived in the House From Hell
and Jesus had no key.

But other someones – people in flesh –
came to save my soul
from the bottomless blackened hole
with flashlights between their teeth,

since words were a liability.
Disregarding danger, they came for me
and hauled me off to a place
that wasn't safe or sane or sanitary,
so I fit right in.
They simply let me be as me –
no agenda for change, but absolutely no abuse,
for they were religious atheists,
escapees from tradition and Bible Drills
and better than/worse thans,
no pledge allegiance to faiths,
but faithful to God alone.

They were secret spies for Jesus
following forgotten failures loved by God
for whom trust was a four-letter word,
whose only chance to meet the God of grace
was through other goats like them
led by a goatherd who didn't act like God,
but was kind and gentle, protective and safe
for the stupid to follow home.

He was Jesus disguised for Halloween,
minus tricks with treats.
He made me laugh, unfaced himself,
then laughed with me, not at me –
what a shock!
He said,

*Dump in the trash what you know about me
and meet me now for real.*

He's not as advertised –
not hateful, but hope-filled,
happy to save us from lies
which are sins against the many,
most-likely dupes to be deceived.

But God's #1 priority
is to ransom the rascal in all of us,
crack a gap the universe wide
between religion and reality
so those riddled by righteousness

have the chance to fall into grace –
a place of acceptance, forgiveness,
with re-birthed lives
and flashlights flossed between teeth.

Chapter 17

We Are The Church

What is the Body of Christ? All believers in Jesus. Whether we like another Jesus-follower or not, we're in the same tribe together. And we need all of us. God has assigned each of us a position, a body part. We don't have to do our part, but whenever any of us play dead, the rest of us suffer from the loss.

I'm pretty good at English, but math is a language I don't understand, and I have school grades to prove it. Math and English majors need each other in our world. None of us is the position to say to anyone else,

> *The eye cannot say to the hand, "I have no need of you";*
> *or again the head to the feet, "I have no need of you." 1*
> *Corinthians 12:21 (NASB)*

Eyes can function just fine without toenails, even though I don't know the purpose of toenails, but God does because He gave them to us. Here's what God says about toenails in the church:

> *On the contrary, it is much truer that the members of the body which seem to be weaker are necessary; and those members of the body which we deem less honorable, on these we bestow more abundant honor, and our less presentable members become much more presentable, whereas our more presentable members have no need of it. But God has so composed the body, giving more abundant honor to that member which lacked, so that there may be no division in the body, but that the members may have the same care for one another. 1 Corinthians 12:22-25 (NASB)*

It has to do with pride. Whenever I feel I'm better or more important than someone else, God says, *"Not so. This is your cue to show respect to a person who doesn't get enough, because they're just as precious and valuable to me as you are."*

I'm active in Kairos Prison Ministry, an ecumenical group of Christians who show and tell Christ's love to inmates in prisons. Incarcerated men and women have been locked up by a judge, but continue to be judged everyday by people in the free world who feel no kindness or mercy should be extended to them, now or ever.

I learned a lot about the Body of Christ serving in prison. I felt more kinship with the inmates than what I called "the nice church ladies" on my team, an unfair judgment on my part that came from incidents of criticism of my past and present by church members. I found out early on what the hot buttons were, and did my best to keep them undercover around Christians in general. I've had all I want of being burned at the stake.

Living by the code of "What they don't know won't hurt me" protected me from abuse to a certain extent, but it also kept me from seeing what I have in common with other believers. It kept me from partnering with them and Jesus in living out love before the people in our universe, and it also cut me off from knowing the blessing of giving and receiving. I had responded to prejudice with prejudice, me against you, whoever you are, whether you're guilty of wounding me or not, merely on the possibility that you might hurt me.

I am so very grateful to the people who have shown me love while I fought them off, who accepted my warped self as is, drawing me into their circle and refusing to accept my complacency. They invited me to the banquet, then threw me a towel, telling me to dry the dishes. In those major acts of love, I found I belonged, and want to help other people find their place in the family of God, too.

Several years ago, Bud was almost killed when a drunk driver t-boned his truck at 100 mph. A total stranger stopped immediately and pulled my unconscious, gravely injured husband out of the burning truck. Miracle number one was Bud surviving the crash. Miracle number two was the man saving Bud's life (he received a civic award for the good deed).

At the time, Bud was self-employed in the home improvement field. His injuries permanently put him out of business. For a year and a half Bud was out of work and spent the first twelve months in a wheelchair. I made $9.00 an hour. Thankfully, we had good medical insurance through my job. We didn't qualify for any government help, and had three teenagers. Things looked bleak.

Then the Body of Christ came to the rescue. Our church knew about the situation, and to people who asked us what they could do to help, we unashamedly asked for money.

For the next two years, the miracles kept coming, not only from church, but also from many other friends. Checks arrived in the mail. Bags of groceries were left at the carport door. Our family helped us in so many ways, including paying our mortgage. About twice a month, the finance secretary at church called and asked me to come pick up a check from one or more anonymous donors. All of our needs were met.

For people with a strong work ethic, it's very hard to receive help. But through this experience we learned a spiritual principle and the purpose of the Body of Christ:

> *My God will supply all your needs according to His riches in glory in Christ Jesus. Philippians 4:19 (NASB)*
>
> *Give, and it will be given to you. A good measure, pressed down, shaken together and running over, will be poured into your lap. For with the measure you use, it will be measured to you. Luke 6:38 (NIV)*

We are the church. We are family. Never take that for granted, and remember your responsibility to actively play your important part. Even if you're a toenail, we need you.

In this chapter, I assert that God calls the church to be the Body of Christ – a composite of believers, merged into a family because God has adopted us as His children, with Jesus as not only our savior, but our brother. As Jesus-followers, we are members of God's universal church, whether we participate or not. Together, we are much more effective in reflecting God's love and mercy within our own realm of influence, while encouraging and supporting each other. We are the church together, living into the kingdom of God.

Fellow Survivors

The bottom crumbles underfoot
into the bottomless below and I waver…
effortlessly drawn to oblivion – the Great Known –
that chasm of despair that desires all the hope in me.
Yet I'm tethered to the prayers and stares
of those stubborn enough
to take the exodus with me out of seeming security
into fifty years of desert,
fellow survivors who won't let go of me
nor their own hope of healing.

For we are not whole alone
and were not, even before the Fall.
I'm stronger broken with missing pieces of me
replaced by part of you,
fused with grace and love from Christ
that I cannot sabotage,
cannot remove nor improve, no matter what –
the invisible bridge that supports me
whether I step or fall.

Crazy God

I've always known I don't color outside the box.
I AM outside the box, made crazy by life,
both by my choices and things done unto me.
I never knew that made in your image
means you're the craziest of all.
I mean, you saved a wrench like me.
It's incomprehensible you made me,
knowing how I'd turn out –
a scrambled egg, a train wreck in the news
with faithless faith to follow you,
though you always follow me.

I look at the saints in churches
comforted by all the bells and whistles,
rites that bring relief to them,
that love you as much as me.
I'm not talking about the pretentious –
attending by habit to earn respectability.
Those who seek your heart with hope,
or want it desperately, know my heart, too,
but I feel we're alien from each other.
Someone who stole a pencil in third grade
fits in a different body of Christ.

But you say we are the church,
all of us, who crave your compassion
the same, but differently.
We know that stars and slugs
bring you equal delight.
It's us with standards of good and bad,
categories of better and worse.
But you're crazy enough to love us all,
to know we're all sinners and saints.

The pencil criminals were made for those
without a mother's love
who just need hugging and acceptance
to find for themselves our mothering God.
You bring catastrophes to me
because I struggle still with defeat and despair,
depression, shame that hasn't healed,

addiction in the present tense.
Catastrophes don't relate to victory.
My commonality with professional losers
helps them hear my God through me,
which shocks me every time
and gives me the same faith I give away.

God is more diverse
than his creation will ever be.
We're fractured facets of his reflection,
fragments that fit into his whole
that fits the hole in me exactly.
It's crazy –
the perfect God needs me.

The Body of Christ

If church is the communion of saints,
then where do you take the ache
that's more than married or buried,
sick of surface, safe responsive readings,
of ritual greetings in communal chorus
where truth be known, but not told,
where it's safe to say the answer
but not the question.

When did Psalm 38 fall out of the hymnal?
Whose choir still sings Psalm 69?
Did I miss the deadline to question Jesus?
The disciples did everyday
and got away with being their silly selves,
for He liked them "as was"
and loved them into passionate givers
of grace that dominoed down to me.

And I bring my piece of the Body of Christ
to church for Show and Tell,
but it tends to stay in my purse
while I wait for someone else to go first.

But invariably, God in me escapes
to dance down the aisles and
whispers during the sermon.
He drops my defenses with people watching
while I try unsuccessfully not to cry
or care about these people
I don't want to know me,
who brought aches up their sleeves
along with their talents,
fears in the envelopes next to their tithes,
their own puzzle pieces safe in their pockets
that only need your piece and mine
to complete the image of God,
a functional family where whores become priests
and nice older people have Jesus in common
with rap-filled teens and crap-filled babies,
where we're magnetized toward people unlike us
who share the same ravenous God-need hunger

for intimate empathy, real communion
with Jesus incarnate at the Lord's table,
at Starbucks and Krogers,
on the top tier balcony and front row of choir.

The thing I fear most
is to give you what I want –
to refuse the generic, which costs less,
and ask for the real,
say what's really wrong
when I want understanding,
counter rudeness with kindness
and un-shroud Christ in my eyes and reactions
to alter the average,
make holy the humblest cup of water
I offer to God
by giving to you the time to listen,
respect as you are,
following God out of safe into saving,
numinous, passionate joy.

Epilogue - Reflections Of A Wrestler

Wrestling with God in Uncensored Prayer is worship – intimate, honest engagement with our Lord, Creator, Savior, and Daddy. God's holiness brings wholeness into our entire being the more time we consciously spend with Him. Scripture says,

> *Pray without ceasing.* 1 Thessalonians 5:17 (NASB)

Another way to say that is,

> *Never stop praying.* 1 Thessalonians 5:17 (NLT)

Obviously, we can't pray constantly, doing nothing else. But I think it means never hanging up the phone with God.

Practice doesn't make perfect (whoever wrote that was lying to themselves). But practice makes what you're doing easier. The more I pray, the more I pray. Today, prayer is the first thing that pops out of my mouth in sudden moments. I catch a fumbled coffee mug before it hits the floor – "Thank you, God." There's a harried mother with a screaming baby in line ahead of me at the store – "God, help that poor woman" and "God, shut the baby up, OK?" I get a third notice on a bill I paid two months ago – "What is wrong with these people? I just want to strangle them," I rant and rave to God, pouring out my frustration.

I've discovered that it's OK to ask God anything, like why He allows tsunamis and genocide. Those conversations eventually get around to the real topic: what God does or allows to happen to me sometimes seems cruel, not loving. For God to say everything He does is based on love seems like crap, like *He's* the one with His head in the sand. When we are willing to bring these questions to God, we can learn that He always has our best interests at heart, even though we may not understand His methods or timing.

Wrestling with God doesn't always mean it's God I'm fighting. Many times when I talk with God, I'm wrestling with myself. He's very biased toward me, but being God, he also has 20/20 vision and perfect perspective. There's only so long God will allow me to beat myself up in His presence. He accepts me as I am, then asks me to follow Him, usually out of my comfort zone.

God knows I always have issues in my life about *something*. When I'm angry, if I take it out on God first, I have a chance to vent and cool down before talking with my adversary. We never have to worry about upsetting God, wishing we hadn't said something we can't take back. Sometimes I can only scream at Him, sniffle, then say, "Thanks for listening." Other times, I can calm down enough to hear God's suggestions, wisdom, and understanding. Any time we come to God, it's win/win.

Sometimes I have used some non-traditional prayer language when I've been angry or hurt. Rather than a lecture, His response has been, "Hooray!" I was being real – ugly and beautiful and everything in between. Be yourself with God and stop editing. You'll get a whole lot more out of your private time together.

Surrendering to God doesn't mean piously lying down on the railroad track, willing for God the Train to run over us. Part of turning our wills and lives over to God means accepting His challenge and fighting with Him over all our questions, fears, even anger toward Him.

We have to go for broke with God in the dirt to find out for ourselves, and I want you to know you will discover more about God and about yourself, which will include respect. It doesn't necessarily mean answers to what we want to know. But what I receive from wrestling with God is a sense of OKness, whether I get the answer I want, or even any answer at all.

Knowing, really knowing God accepts me as I am has ended up being more important to me than peace. Knowing God is going to take care of me and my situation has been enough for me, even if it lasts five minutes, because I know I can go right back to God and tell Him how I feel about it.

God wants us to get alone with Him, so that we can talk with Him honestly without interruption. To do that, we have to take the initiative to seek God and ask for His help. Taking the risk to do this requires the willingness to face truth about ourselves, which is often painful. The pay-off is the relief God offers – we no longer have to bear our burdens alone, and in the process, God grants us peace from experiencing His forgiveness and compassion.

Hiding from truth costs us freedom from the barriers that separate us from God and ourselves. We all believe lies about who God really is and our self-worth. It's easy for us to think that we aren't good enough for God, even if that's unconscious. Also, we tend to evaluate ourselves based on comparisons to other people: "She's so much prettier than me;" "He's such a success, and I can't measure up."

God wants us to know that we are precious and valuable just as we are, and to believe the truth of that, we have to spend time with God, discovering who He really is, laying aside assumptions and previous training. God always affirms us, and as we participate with God in Uncensored Prayer, we can let go of lies and dishonesty, and discover for ourselves that truth is liberating and wonderful.

One of our greatest desires is for healing from all the deep wounds in our hearts. If we think God is one of those who has hurt us, it's hard to come to Him, because He may hurt us again. Jacob chose to wrestle with God when his pain was more than he could bear, and he felt he had nothing left to lose. Sometimes we have to be desperate to take the risk that talking honestly with God can make a difference, and sometimes God allows us to reach that place of despair without any relief from Him so that we will seek Him on our own, and discover the healing that only God can bring.

There are other costs of wrestling with God. Pride has to go, because it's an attempt to be God, which we can't do. Our pride that we are self-sufficient is due to fail at some point, and to deny this is destructive to both our relationship with God and ourselves. A willingness to lay aside our pride and fear that God might not accept us as we are, faults and all, takes courage and faith that reaching out to God might be worth the cost. The only way for us to find out is to try it.

Another difficult thing is stepping out of the comfort zone of our spiritual traditions to see if God might have more for us – new and fresh ways of experiencing Him. God encourages and honors every spiritual practice that accurately reveal Him, but He always wants us to follow Him into the unknown, resulting in growth and an enriched life.

To do this means confronting the fear of what other people might think, especially the possibility of criticism from those close to us. As we discover that God loves and likes us as we are, we can lay aside hiding behind lies to cover who we really are. Fear of abandonment is common to us all. Coming to know God's unconditional acceptance of us through unedited conversations with Him allows us to accept ourselves, regardless of other's opinions.

Through honest conversations with God we find that He is interested in everything about us, and listens respectfully to all we say. He also teaches us how to hear from Him through a variety of ways. As we become aware of God's messages to us, we will hear God speaking to us personally more and more – an incredible, encouraging thing. The Holy God of the universe wants to converse *with* us – a two-way street. What an awesome privilege!

Gideon was a great Biblical example of someone wrestling with God in Uncensored Prayer. He didn't hesitate to complain to God and test Him.

> *The angel of the LORD appeared to him and said to him,*
> *"The LORD is with you, O valiant warrior."*

> *Then Gideon said to him, "O my lord, if the LORD is with us, why then has all this happened to us? And where are all His miracles which our fathers told us about, saying, 'Did not the LORD bring us up from Egypt?' But now the LORD has abandoned us and given us into the hand of Midian." Judges 6:12-13 (NASB)*

God had a job in mind for Gideon – He wanted Gideon to deliver Israel from the Midianites, and promised to be with him. Gideon wanted proof; God's promise wasn't enough for him. So God performed a miracle.

> *The angel of God said to him, "Place the meat and the unleavened bread on this rock, and pour the broth over it."*
> *And Gideon did as he was told. Then the angel of the LORD touched the meat and bread with the tip of the staff in his*

> hand, and fire flamed up from the rock and consumed all he had brought. *Judges 6:20-21 (NLT)*

Apparently miracles didn't impress Gideon. He wanted another.

> Gideon said to God, "If you will save Israel by my hand as you have promised – look, I will place a wool fleece on the threshing floor. If there is dew only on the fleece and all the ground is dry, then I will know that you will save Israel by my hand, as you said." And that is what happened. Gideon rose early the next day; he squeezed the fleece and wrung out the dew – a bowlful of water. *Judges 6:36-38 (NIV)*

Two miracles didn't convince Gideon. He was a hard sell.

> Then Gideon said to God, "Do not be angry with me. Let me make just one more request. Allow me one more test with the fleece, but this time make the fleece dry and let the ground be covered with dew." That night God did so. Only the fleece was dry; all the ground was covered with dew. *Judges 6:39-40 (NIV)*

God's patience with this guy astounds me until I remember the tests I've put Him through. God knows we tend to be stubborn, manipulative, and selfish. I think He enjoys the challenge when we wrestle with Him, because we're at least playing ball together. If one person has a bat and someone else has a ball, and then one of them goes home, there's no game.

The same thing applies to God and us. We won't hear Him unless we listen. We can't get to know Him and learn from Him unless we spend time with Him. And we'll never grow spiritually unless we give God all we've got, which means not only surrender but conflict. Remember, God didn't rename Jacob until they fought all night. God was so impressed with Jacob's audacity that he got a new name and identity out of it.

> And He said, Your name shall be called no more Jacob [supplanter], but Israel [contender with God]; for you have contended and have power with God and with men and have prevailed. *Genesis 32:28 (AMP)*

It's a great compliment when God changes your name to "Fought With God and Won." Won what? You have to find out for yourself.

Practical Applications

God knows everything about us and what we think. So why does He want us to engage in the spiritual practice of Uncensored Prayer? To be completely honest with God, we first have to be truthful with ourselves, which may be difficult or unpleasant. Jacob became willing to take the risk of wrestling with God out of a deep heart's desire to reconcile with his brother, and a longing to have his life changed. He was tired of handling his problems alone, which didn't work. He wanted a personal encounter with God more than continuing to play it safe, following a comfortable path that didn't fully satisfy the longing in his soul to really matter. Little did he know that wrestling with God with all he had would change his life forever for the good. Through this painful encounter with God, Jacob was blessed far beyond anything he could have imagined.

Would you like such a transformational relationship with God for yourself? God longs for a bond of love and trust with us not possible with anyone else. He offers this blessing to each of us, but we must seek Him with all our heart. God promises that

Those who seek me find me. Proverbs 8:17 (NIV)

The LORD is near to all who call on him, to all who call on him in truth. Psalm 145:18 (NIV)

Do you want to try the spiritual practice of wrestling with God and Uncensored Prayer? Here are some exercises to help you get started. There are no right or wrong answers. Write down the truth. Just find out where you are. That's where you have to begin before moving forward. Ask God to help you.

Uncensored Prayer

1. Are you hesitant to try Uncensored Prayer? If so, why?
2. How do you currently pray? Do you recite the Lord's Prayer at church or in a 12 Step group? Read prayers out of a book? Kneel in church or by your bed at night? Pray with your eyes closed or open? Only pray in church, outside, in privacy, or wherever you are? Fold your hands or raise your hands in the air? Pray silently or out loud? Let someone else do your praying for you? Not pray at all?
3. What have you always wanted to *ask* God?
4. What have you always wanted to *say* to God?
5. Are you afraid that God won't accept you as you are? Why?
6. Do you fear God has conditions you aren't certain you meet? If so, what are they?
7. How do you view God? Is He distant? Loving or judgmental? Unwilling to listen to you because of your past, present, or whatever? Is God holy to you or a jerk? Is He an intimate friend, acquaintance, or a stranger?
8. If you could have any kind of God you want, what would He/She be like?
9. Pick a word or phrase you think is inappropriate to use in prayer, but that you say a lot to other people, then use it while talking to God.
10. Write down an uncensored prayer to God in your own words. Change the way you're comfortable praying. For example, if you always end your prayers with, "In Jesus' name", don't do it this time. Then read your prayer out-loud.
11. Try praying with your eyes open.
12. Try changing your prayer posture. If you have never done so, kneel to pray or stand up.
13. Pray in a different location from your usual spot, such as while driving (unless it distracts you), outside, in the shower.

14. Sing your prayer (remember, you're alone. God doesn't care what you sound like). Don't try to figure out a melody, just sing your prayer.
15. Are you angry about something right now? Tell God about it.
16. Are you angry at *God* right now? Tell Him. Don't hold back. He won't be offended.
17. What have you never told anyone? Tell God. He will neither judge you nor shame you, plus He'll keep your confidence.
18. Sit still with yourself alone and practice meditation. Prayer is talking to God; meditation is listening to God. Listen to your heart, and with your heart. Think about God – all that He is, all that He has done for you. Have no expectations.

    "Be still, and know that I am God." Psalm 46:10 (NLT)

    I will meditate with my heart, and my spirit ponders. Psalm 77:6 (NAS)

    I will meditate on all Your work and muse on Your deeds. Psalm 77:12 (NAS)

    I will meditate on Your precepts and regard Your ways. Psalm 119:15 (NAS)

19. Think of how you talk with your best friend or the person closest to you. Try talking to God like that.
20. Write a prayer poem to God. It doesn't matter if you have never written a poem. You've read my poems, and I just talk to God in them. You can do this.

As you practice wrestling God through Uncensored Prayer, you will discover the way of talking with God that is comfortable for you, and find Him speaking to you in many different ways.

I pray you will be blessed by this book, and have your experience with God renewed or started. Feel free to contact me with comments, and to arrange speaking engagements, interviews, and guest blog posts. You can reach me at: joyleewilson@g.mail.com.

Other Books By Civitas Press

The Practice of Love: Real Stories of Living Into Kingdom of God, Edited by Jonathan Brink

This collection of stories explores a remarkably simple idea. What would it look like to practice love? What would happen if we actively chose to engage a deep sense of love even in hard places? The possibilities include a love for God, a love for the self, a love for a neighbor, and even a love for an enemy. What emerges will inspire and challenge the reader to reconsider what it means to live out the practice of love in our lives.

Retail: $15.99 | 294 Pages

Down We Go: Living Into the Wild Ways of Jesus by Kathy Escobar

Down We Go is a practitioner's guide for creating and cultivating missional community. It's based on the idea of living into the Beatitudes, and explores what it means to follow Jesus into the hard places of suffering, inequality, and injustice in order to cultivate, hope, beauty, justice, equality, generosity and healing.

Retail: $15.99 | 278 Pages

Broken By Religion, Healed By God: Restoring the Evangelical, Sacramental, Pentecostal, Social Justice Church by Gordon Dalbey

Best-selling author Gordon Dalbey's newest book explores the much needed healing in the church. In the Bible, Jesus reveals Himself in four major ways, each of which has been claimed by a larger Christian faction: the born-again experience, by Evangelicals; eucharist/communion, by Sacramentalists; the baptism of the Holy Spirit, by Pentecostals, and social justice ministry, by Oldline Reformers. Instead of celebrating each other's vision to know Jesus more fully, each of the four have discounted the others and thereby, crippled the Church.

Retail: $14.99 | 286 Pages

Made in the USA
Charleston, SC
13 May 2012